Grace Notes and Other Fragments

JOSEPH A. SITTLER

Grace Notes
and Other Fragments

Selected and Edited by
ROBERT M. HERHOLD
and
LINDA MARIE DELLOFF

FORTRESS PRESS   Philadelphia

Library of Congress Cataloging in Publication Data

Sittler, Joseph.
    Grace notes and other fragments.

    1. Theology—Collected works—20th century.
2. Lutheran Church—Collected works. I. Title.
BT15.S585   230'.41   80-8055
ISBN 0-8006-1406-6

8267F80   Printed in the United States of America   1-1404

For
Jeanne, Stephen, Joseph IV,
Edward, Barbara, Philip, and Bay

Contents

Preface

The grace note in music can be dispensed with. It does not carry the main melody; it is not necessary to complete the structure. But it has, withal, a function. It accents a beat, underlines a moving turn of melody, freshens a phrase, gives vivacity to something well-known.

Among the large facts and the grand events of life we can hear the small grace notes of the gospel's meaning. The reflections, essays, and fragments in this book seek only to record some of these fleeting notes that sound, sometimes, alongside the larger music of our lives like small ornaments of insight.

They were collected by my admired friend, the Reverend Robert M. Herhold of Palo Alto, California. With a good nose for such pieces as I have written over the years, and from taped interviews, he selected those which in his judgment might be of interest and use to a variety of readers. Because I am madly careless about files and a champion misplacer of papers, this task was a formidable one. Pastor Herhold scrounged about with angelic patience, and I am heartily grateful to him.

It is also a happy task to thank Linda Marie Delloff, associate editor of *The Christian Century*, for undertaking the copy-editing of the book with characteristic patience and good humor, and with a sure eye for grammar, diction, proper sequence, logic, and allusions sometimes left hanging. Ms. Delloff has forced all such details to shape up.

JOSEPH A. SITTLER
Chicago
Third week of Lent, 1980

Christmas

In an older day Christmas came with a special splash of wonder. Around December 15 there arrived at the church wooden buckets of teeth-rotting candies, which the Ladies Aid secretly packed in dozens of gaily colored little boxes with white string handles. At the inevitable and memorable children's program on the Sunday afternoon before Christmas, these were distributed to the youngsters. The excitement of that little box is impossible to recapture in our year-round candy culture.

At the program each child had a "piece" to say. For some it was a grand moment. For others it was a terror; Mother had to sit in the front row and be ready to supply the forgotten line (in a whisper that reached the farthest corner).

The high point, of course, was the angels. Cheesecloth-clad and tinsel-haloed little girls, all agiggle, were everywhere. What actual angels wear we do not know; in the Christmas program they always wore white cotton stockings (which tended to bunch at the knees and had regularly to be hitched up).

Boys seldom made the angel ranks. Instead they played wise men (in costumes borrowed from the local Elks, Masons, Moose, Knights of Pythias, or some other brotherhood). Or they were shepherds—whose costumes presented no problem: beat-up bathrobes were always available. Scotch-plaid patterns (which would have been astonishing to first-century sheepherders) were especial favorites. I remember one mad moment when I was a shepherd in the Christmas pageant; I had forgotten to take the cigars out of the bathrobe borrowed from my uncle. Father saw the brightly banded cigars sticking out of the breast pocket and snatched them just before our entrance to keep "watch over the flocks by night."

Many families, at Christmastime, were hosts to a once-a-year visit by an old grandfather or other relative who came along to the program, and was sometimes a lurid character. I remember my grandfather. He was always in sober broadcloth, white vest, an elk's tooth suspended from a gold chain across the imposing frontal expanse, exuding a most unchristian aroma of one-hundred-proof bourbon over the entire congregation. He gave each child in the family a polished half-dollar. But he too stood with the others. And he too, perhaps remembering more innocent days and ways, sang out with everyone else who was there,

> How silently, how silently
> The wondrous gift is given!

How blended, in Christian faith, are the simple and the sublime; how strangely is the profound transmitted by the ordinary; how quickly crumples the pompous ostentation of our lives before the primal pure; how powerful is the clear, bright blade of amazing grace as it flashes again amid all forgettings, denials, sheer clutterings.

Gawking and Enjoying

I think the assumption that first you must know yourself and then you decide what to do with yourself is a fundamental blunder. The truth of the matter is that one does not know himself or herself. That's a false conclusion because the self is not an isolated entity. The self is constituted by its relationships, and the only self-knowledge we can have is the knowledge that comes by virtue of the self existing among other selves.

People frequently ask me how to find and know the self. Let me be quite personal. In my reflection, I have come to the surprising conclusion that I have never asked that question; it seems to be a traumatic one for many, but it has never been of concern to me. In a sense, I have been greatly blessed by having had a modest self-image as a child. I had a very smart older brother and a very beautiful older sister. I was just a third kid, and therefore I would simply open my eyes and look around and gawk and enjoy whatever there was to enjoy. By never asking who I was, I developed a self without pressing the question.

Young people often come to me and say: "I may drop out of school or leave this place or quit my job. I've got to go off by myself and find out who I am." Well, I can understand the pathos of the situation and what motivates their feeling, and I can be patient with their convictions. At the same time, I'm very dubious as to success. There's a poem by Theodore Roethke that says,

> I wake to sleep, and take my waking slow. . . .
> I learn by going where I have to go.

You find that your self emerges more quickly if you do not keep scratching the question. If you lose your life, you find it, or it could be that it will find you. You will say, "Now that seems to be what I am, or what I'd like to do." I don't think you go to some sterile, barren land filled with sagebrush and gaze at your navel to find out who you are.

Eleanor and the Big Brown Buick

The other day I went to Marshall Field's department store to pick up a wedding gift. As I entered on the State Street side, I passed that first counter where they display the cosmetics and perfumes; clerks are always squirting this stuff at you. Suddenly I had a whiff of something I had not encountered for fifty years. A certain girl named Eleanor had worn that scent when we borrowed her brother's big brown Buick and went off for a hamburger near Plymouth, Ohio.

Eleanor is now somewhere in Texas, her brother is gone, I am sure the Buick is gone, and I am damned-near gone. But after fifty years, that scent took me right back to the brown Buick and Eleanor and all the rest of it, which was considerable.

I think everyone has had some such experience: a chance sniff, the feel of some object, a respoken word or line that one has not heard since the eighth grade. There is something in the associational, in what we call the infinite retrievability of the past. It is embedded in the senses, in the chemistry, in the cerebrum somehow; it makes computers look simple.

No Mathematics of Providence

I have never found it possible to lay down a program regarding the apparitions of the providence of God. I look at my own life and I cannot be absolutely sure that the things that have happened to me, that seemed to be positive and useful, had a direct line to God's providence. Some of these seemed to have been accidental. I was in the right place at the right time, and I happened to have been studying a subject just when somebody wanted something said about it. Maybe that's the way the providence of God works, but I have no mathematics of providence. I feel that I have been providentially led, in that I had motivations I cannot fully understand.

For reasons that have nothing to do with Christian commitment, I have always been interested in nature and I just kept acting on that interest, not out of a service to God but because I enjoyed it. Then I found that what I did for enjoyment served well to help me relate theology to the environmental problem. That may be the way God gets his providential things done; and I hope it is. But I don't want to stick him with it. You know, people often tell me, "Now I will make this decision, I will pray about it." I must say (not with pride, because it's nothing to be proud of) that I don't pray about such things. When I was called to the University of Chicago, what I did was come down here for one brief quarter and try it out before making my answer to the invitation. Then I woke up one day to discover that inwardly I had already accepted the invitation. There was a thing to be done here; I felt competent to do it; it needed doing; it was worth doing.

Walking

Not always but often, boredom is simply the emotional underside of insensitivity. Think of how Walt Whitman could ride the Staten Island Ferry and write ecstatic poetry about the variety of life in the New York Harbor. He could walk the streets of old Brooklyn and write about the sheer indestructibility of human courage and gallantry—and hence of life. Now we live in the midst of a Hollywood culture. We have been so oversensated by extravaganzas that we have lost the capacity for the delicate, the nuance, the small things. I know of no solution to this problem except the one that St. Francis found in his century. Maybe the world must disappear into the tunnel and divest itself of what it thought constituted liberating, free, vivacious life; then strip away the last rags of sensation and learn to look again at the simple.

The first time I took a train through the desert, I thought it was an endless expanse of brown gravel. Then someone took me on a walk there. I saw countless miniature flowers and plants. Up close, the lichen on the gray rock had a hundred colors.

When we go on wheels, we miss what can be seen only on foot. I am always mentioning to various friends who are sedentary and auto-trapped riders the things I see walking in my Chicago neighborhood—things they never see because they whiz past them in a car. There are exquisite ironworks, beautiful little stone carvings, lovely doorways. I can point out so many fascinating details because I walk. We rush through life and see the panoramic, but miss the microscopic.

Marriage and Snow on the Mountain

The heart of marriage is a promise. On the face of it, it's a crazy promise: two people who have only a partial understanding of each other stand up and make this bizarre statement that they're going to cherish and care for one another for a lifetime. They say, "I take this one and this one takes me as long as we both shall live," not "as long as we both shall love." To many persons this seems like a mad and risky thing to do. Yet I would suggest that the madness is the romance. Without risk there is no beauty or strength or goodness.

It's not a very courageous thing for two people who have found themselves mutually delectable to say, "We will shack up as long as the delectability continues." That's neither broadly human nor is it particularly commendable. It has no gallantry. It's a mutual opportunism. So that if people want to create all kinds of lovely music about what is simply one of the higher forms of self-satisfaction, I find nothing admirable about this at all. I find it completely understandable. I find it even momentarily delightful. But I don't think it has much to do with marriage. Certainly nothing to do with a promise. I'm really challenged toward fulfillment only when I understand marriage as the mutual acceptance of a challenge to fulfill the seemingly impossible. Then there is something that is really worth the human effort.

Bach produced greatness within the strict musical limits of his time; indeed, the severity of the limits called forth the magnificence of the accomplishment. Just as Bach accepted limitations and discipline in musical composition, so marriage means limits. Without limitation there is no expansion. Without the risk of a promise there is no true joy. There is only a kind of serial, episodic history of partial joys with inter-changeable parts.

The problem with the temporary, ad hoc relationships which many people enter into today is that when there is a way out, the couple deprive themselves of the deepening effect of going all the way in. When there's an exit, they can split. This is not to say that all marriages should survive. Sometimes the damage done in staying together is so great that the only answer is a dissolution; we all know marriages like that.

It does not fit today's popular mood, but we all need fidelity: the intention to do what we say, to accept discipline in order to solidify the good. Fidelity means more than not sleeping around the neighborhood. It means that we have made a promise, a commitment, and that we have accepted the limitations that are a part of that promise. There are great satisfactions in saying, "I have done what I undertook to do."

In marriage people may have differences and periods of weariness and boredom, but they have also built up an axis of relationships that constitutes a steady center. And if you take that away, life becomes intolerable. I may have such difficulty with my wife that I don't want to talk to her, but if she isn't home when she ought to be, I'm troubled. As a friend said, "At least there is someone around whom I don't want to talk to."

There's a story by Flannery O'Connor in which she tells about an old couple who had lived in the Appalachians all their lives in a little cabin overlooking the opposite mountain. They were sitting there—both very aged people—in their rocking chairs on a spring day. The man said, "Well, Sarah, I see there's still some snow up there on the mountain." Now he knew there was snow on the mountain every year. She knew there was snow every year. So why does he have to say it? Because to perceive that, to know that at times there is snow and at times there is not snow—this was part of the observation of an eternal rhythm which made their life together. In marriage you say the same things over and over, you inquire about the same poeple; and this is ho-hum in one way. But it is breathtaking in another.

No Substitute for an Act

There is no substitute for an act. For instance, our churchyard was a nondescript half-city-lot. We didn't make any big announcement; three of us just started to clean it up and set in some plantings. Then other people said, "I'll come over next Saturday to help you." Or they said, "I admire you heartily, but I'm too weak to dig; here's ten bucks."

Pleasure and Piety

My trip here to Oregon is a combination of pleasure and piety.
I'm doing what I like to do—that is the pleasure. I'm doing
what I ought to do—that is the piety.

A Late Sunday Night Ride
on the El

Late Sunday night . . . the long, dull ride on the elevated train returning to campus from an Easter appointment. There they sat, or slumped, over early editions of the next morning's paper, or swayed from straps: the people! The people, who are for the gospel's awakening stab or healing touch in our day what "the multitudes" were in Jesus' day.

Each of these is a person. Each has a name, a personal history —and dignity. In the great milling world each is a digit in a statistical total; behind the eyes of each is the incommunicable loneliness of the self. The faces, the gestures and attitudes and the pathos of ultimate insulation that blurs personality . . .

But the blur is never absolute. A girl sits wrapped in a bright red coat, the marks and creases of its yesterday newness still fresh upon it. She no doubt works in one of the Loop's vast animal-cage offices, and she saved her money for this Easter Day fling on Michigan Avenue in her pretty red coat. She's so small there, squeezed into the corner seat. Not so small or so squeezed, though, but remains still in her new coat a bright individual. She's proud and has a secret all to herself, and her eyes glow above her weak, childlike chin.

Across the car another girl, who tries to hide the mystery of the individual behind a mask of the magazine-cover face that tends to make all pretty girls look alike. She has dark, well-groomed hair, lovely coloring, a clear and handsome forehead. Self-possessed, assured (like the photos of the North Shore girls in the Sunday supplement that's crumpled in her lap)—she wears a very cool and too-old, knowing look. But the ingenuous white, fuzzy mittens dissolve the role. And her feet are unconsciously turned in at a little-girl angle, shod in casual loafers that seem to talk back to the anonymity of her bearing:

"Come now, would-be woman of the world! The quietness behind that too-knowing face is something else again."

And that neat, prim, little clerk of a man in the next seat. His head is tilted at an awkward angle so that his eyes can strike the paper just right for his bifocals. He would melt into the general grayness of the crowd but for a great, gaudy, ruby tiepin! *His* word, perhaps, to all the world—his private defiance flung out to the nameless, trampling thousands on the streets: "Oh, you *would*, would you!" Here is a person too, and he has a ruby in his tie!

Do you remember? "I have called thee by *thy name*—thou art mine!" . . . and with a loud voice one cried, "What have I to do with thee, Jesus, thou Son of God most high! I beseech thee, torment me not." And Jesus asked him, saying, *"What is your name?"* Or this: "Thou art *Peter"* . . . indubitably and indelibly *thyself!* A *person!* And the infinitude of longing and love that yet speaks to us in Jesus' quiet, searching repetition of a loved name . . . Simon . . . Martha, Martha . . .

Our gospel is no system, no cold, commanding frame of principles, no general flung-out cry from God to life's masses. It knows each by *name*, calls by *name*, knocks at the door of each one's heart with an urgency and a tenderness born of God's knowledge of each one's solitude. Its destiny and proper home is the person lost in the herded elevated train, furtive and proud in the flaunting red coat, yet lonely in the immaculate solitude behind the too-suave look, timid and frightened behind the bifocals and the ridiculous ruby.

Feet Firmly Planted in Midair

I am always somewhat embarrassed when I am introduced as a systematic theologian, particularly as an eminent one, because I am neither. I am too good a theologian to think I am a great one, and my way of reflection is too nonsequential to deserve the adjective "systematic." A young scholar at the Louvain has written a doctoral dissertation called *Logos and Lord: A Study of the Cosmic Christology of Joseph Sittler*. In a chapter on my theological style the writer says: "With both feet firmly planted in midair, he takes off in several directions." That is probably so. But I justify this method as a way of being a theologian, though not a good way of being a systematic theologian.

I justify my method by an analogy. My grandmother once instructed me when I was quite young about how to clean a spot out of a textile. She said: "When you have a spot you have to remove, do not start rubbing directly on the spot. Start out at the edge and work in from all around because if you rub on the spot, you will get the spot out and leave a ring around it. So you work from the outside in." If I have a theological method, that is it; to walk around the question or the issue or the problem and see it as carefully as I can from several perspectives and then hope that the outcome is useful. Often it is, and often it is not.

Home Base

At seminaries and in schools preparatory to the seminary discipline, I have often been asked by identity-anxious students whether the work appropriate to the ministry will be congruent with their search for identity. My reply is that the contemporary split between identity and commitment is probably a false one. When Gerard Manley Hopkins said, "What I do is me," his statement was earthy and true. For identity is a kind of possibility and promise; it will most often open to the substance and shape of a commitment. Ordination to the ministry fixes one's identity where one's commitments are.

Home base for the location of the ministry is like home base on the baseball field. The players do not decide where home base is. The decision is given in the nature of the game. Whether I knew what home base was when I was preparing for the ministry is doubtful, but upon my ordination I was told. I was ordained to the ministry of the Word of God and of the Sacraments. So in a sense my home base is the church's determination, and the church got that determination from the constitution of the church by the One who was both Base and Home. If that kind of initial objectivity really were to determine our understanding of our ministry, a good deal of the present perturbation about the minister's self-image and the image of the minister by the population at large could be prevented. If one has a given home base and understands that his or her vocation is to play the game from there, one's self-image is a result of how well and devoutly this is accomplished.

I meet so many young people who say they want to train for the ordained ministry "because they want to help people." Helping people is important, but a minister is not ordained to help people in general. He or she is there with an understanding that the ultimate help for people is to put them into relationship with God. Now if the minister extends that help, this will engender other forms of aid which follow upon it and are the expression of it. If one has faith, one will have charity and also an understanding of what kind of help people need to which ordination is a direct access.

Purely for Export

I am what is called a constructive theologian: it is my job to probe at the edges of things as responsibly as I can. But I am not a normative church theologian. I was never a ranking theologian in my own Lutheran Church in America; I was never turned loose here in the United States but was told by the church authorities, "You're purely for export." And this was right in the sense that my theological reflection has always been more exploratory than that of a conserving, transmitting church theologian. I am not a *non*church theologian, but my interest is always in asking: "To what degree is this precious tradition ductile, flexible? To what degree do the images and symbols and the statements intersect modernity in ways which the past has had to investigate?" That is the margin on which I live.

I have always been concerned to do justice to the symbols and formulations of the past, but when I try to go beyond these, my efforts have only the authority which is intrinsic to the appropriateness with which the accumulated past intersects the fresh present. One does not have to agree with Sittler, and many people don't; such disagreement advances a healthy conversation within the church. Indeed, the church must cherish such characters as myself and keep us alive and kicking in order to stimulate its own discomfort and growth. I think this is one of the unintended strengths of the LCA; it has permitted our denomination to sustain a lively internal dialogue. The church authorities have never circumscribed my freedom, but it is interesting that I have delivered lectures in Switzerland and England which I have not been invited to deliver in some LCA schools. Distant waves do less disturb the local shoreline.

27

Heralds Who Have Legs

A live gospel demands live spokespersons. A commanding summons requires heralds who have legs that can move and a disposition to move them. Precise and cutting declaration of the Word requires workers who know how to lay brick, and not merely well-disposed children of church homes who can acquire a general plastering ability with the mortar of a pious phraseology. The mind of this generation is in a whirling tailspin and it can only be addressed savingly from God's side of things by persons who are sensitive, capable of tragic involvement in their generation's torment, eager, curious, more than a little angry with what humans have made of humanity in general, and with what American life has made of its promise and hope in particular.

Anything New in Psalm 23?

Take Psalm 23—who would think one would find anything new there? I was sitting in chapel and I heard the reader say, "Though I walk through the valley of the shadow of death, I will fear no evil . . ." Look at that phrase. You walk through the valley of the *shadow* of death—not the valley of death. The valley of death is constituted by the moment of death itself, but for all of life one walks through a valley over which the *shadow* of death moves. One moves toward death. That is not just rhetoric. "Walk through the valley of the shadow" says that we live toward nonliving; we move toward nonbeing. We move every day toward the moment when we shall not move at all. The whole of life is a valley under the shadow of death, and the only way to celebrate the gravity of life is to know that.

The Sacraments and Mystery

Why, when biblical theology is pointing to the distinctive nature of the Christian faith, the Christian Scriptures, and the Christian cultus, does the church's practice of the Holy Communion remain for the most part unaffected by this reversal? Why, when theology is pressing toward cleaner and clearer ways of distinguishing the Christian message from general religiousness, do our congregational practices in Word and Sacrament show such slight and unexciting influence from these freshly given dimensions of meaning? Why, to put it bluntly, after almost a century of recovered biblical theology with its strong accent on the uniqueness of the Christian faith, does its practice in Word and its celebration in Sacrament so weakly reflect this grace?

I propose that the reason for the failure of carry-over is this: our general congregational life is so deeply sunk in a monodimensional and thoroughly secularized culture as largely to have lost ear, eye, and heart for a word or a deed that asserts a totally *different* possibility. The Sacrament proposes to human need an action of God! Related to human life, to be sure, but ungrounded in it, a strong unconsulted Act which shatters and recreates in a new dimension of meaning all things—this act has a hard time with us. In modern times, the ruthless reduction of structures of significance, the coarsened perception of meaning in nature, in history, and in personal life have left us so spiritually impoverished as to stand before such a possibility either stupidly or impatiently. Our modern life has brought to terrible maturity two threats to the many-dimensioned life of the spirit: a new way of living which has so emptied old permanencies as to make them juiceless shells, and a new mode of working which makes personal activity meaningless for millions, unsustaining to the hungry imagination. When bread is the end product of planting and tilling and nurturing the fields of one's ancestral home, and when wine is the domestic product of vines pruned and cared for by our hands and by the hands of remembered fathers under the suns of home—then heavenly investiture of these common things with divine meaning is a possibility. But such investiture comes very close to becoming an impossibility for a generation that buys its bread in shining wrappers in a supermarket and procures its wine at the corner liquor store.

These ideas point to the only serious and Christian ground for efforts to enrich the liturgical life of the contemporary church. The liturgical enthusiasm of the aesthetes or the ceremonialists simply does not operate on a level sufficiently deep to be of help to us. Liturgical discussions which concern themselves with formal preservation, details of dress and movement, and all the other impassioned agenda-items of the sentimentalist have nothing to offer. What is needed is a concentrated attack on the lost realms of wonder and terror and ambiguity which lie so shallowly beneath the chatty, bland life of our Sunday-morning parish situation—an attack equipped for its work by biblical knowledge, theological acumen, and a shared awareness of the infinite equivocations in the lives of the people who still come, even expectantly, to our churches.

Regard the celebration of the Eucharist in a Roman Church ceremony, or among a congregation of Eastern Orthodox believers. No delineation of theological errors can avail to destroy the impression that here a rite is performed in such a way as to challenge common categories of understanding, usual ways of communication, and to assert that something is happening which is not to be understood from the world's side at all. Everything conspires to assert that a divine mystery, a Holy Presence, is both awaited and offered. Vestments and lights, murmured prayers and recollective words from Psalter and Evangel, solemn movements and grave mien, the tinkling bell and the gestures of adoration and supplication seem to hold up

31

and hold forth something utterly alien to, but invasive of, what is everywhere else available. Only the altar of the church knows this ceremony; only at the Mass is such a drama ever seen.

To many a non-Roman believer, even to one who knows the "abomination of the Mass" to lie in his earthly seizing of the ineffable mystery of God and this dogmatic domestication of the mystery within the control of the hierarchical church—even to such a one there occurs a feeling that something is very *right* about the mood of this divine service, something only infrequently present in his or her own practice of public worship. Analysis can discover the constituents of this feeling; and at the very center is this: that the deed of God in Christ is a divine mystery, that grounding all the comprehensions and formulations of theology is an incomprehensible and bottomless movement of Holy Love.

Regard now the preaching of the Word and the administration of the Sacrament of the Lord's Supper in our evangelical churches. (What is here said is not everywhere so, but is general enough to deserve this inquiry.) The very look and conduct of public worship ill frames the mighty mystery. The mood of the congregation is akin to that of an assembly converging on a concert, a lecture, or a theater. The place does not press people into silence; rather, they invade it with the conversation and manners of the street or the hall. Neither altar lights nor devout prelude dissipate this invasion; it rolls over both like an unbroken tide.

As if it could not abide a single alien cubicle, the world has laid hold of the church and dressed it to its fashion. Hundreds of our bright new churches seem almost frantically to strive to provide a Better Homes and Gardens living room for the Lord God. By the time the decorators have finished, nothing peculiar to what happens or is said in the place is permitted to remain. Everything that might speak the word of a holy difference has been softened down and modified. Nothing is hard, or tough, or uncompromising. The wood is not permitted to retain its natural character but is doped, polished, and finished so that it will look like that used for the paneling in the suburban dress shop. The dossal has its textile antecedents in the shimmering svelteness of the town banker's living room.

There is a richness that speaks of the beauty of holiness; and there is another richness that asserts the theory of the leisure class and the doctrine of conspicuous waste—and the Christian cultus once had the taste to know the difference.

If the place and the manner ill frame a deed whose *difference* is of its essence, the matter of our preaching is worse. How a person can read before the people the tremendous utterances of the Order for Public Confession and then allow a sermon to be a pious puddling around in superficial moralism is difficult to understand. What a thing we dare to say when we read that order! No less is promised than real rescue from the clutch of every perdition that lays waste to life—all the way from ultimate food and drink for those "who humbly confess their sins, and who hunger and thirst after righteousness"—through the demoniac imprisonments "from which we can in no wise set ourselves free"—on to the mighty promise that "whosoever eateth of this Bread and drinketh of this Cup, firmly believing the words of Christ, dwelleth in Christ, and Christ in him, and hath eternal life." In a time when thousands are flocking to hear vigorous advice about how to live longer and enjoy life, surely the Faith-Word about how to live forever and enjoy eternal blessedness with the Fountain of Life should, in its proclamation and offering, elicit at least equal animation.

Liturgy and the Prophetic

I love the liturgical orders of the church. Order, appropriateness, beauty—in music, vestments, the church year, etc. Fine! But these traditions are edifying only when, as before the gravity of the will of God, we use and refine them with what might be called a "holy sense of humor." Chasubles can mask uncharity, and vestments can adorn triviality. These things are *our* inventions and are good and useful. But the old prophet Zechariah, with an axlike sense for the center, put the balance right. When the people ask him whether they ought to change the traditional month of fasting, he ignores the question and shifts the issue from a prissy liturgical detail to the real matter at hand:

> And the word of the Lord came to Zechariah, saying, "Thus says the Lord of hosts, Render true judgments, show kindness and mercy each to his brother, do not oppress the widow, the fatherless, the sojourner, or the poor; and let none of you devise evil against his brother in your heart."
>
> (Zech. 7:8–10)

The Word

There are, there must be times when the preacher lets you down; times when your expectations are disappointed by inexpertness. But may I kindly suggest that there are other times when through the preacher the Word is spoken with clarity and sharpness—but you, expecting nothing beyond "just another sermon," are inattentive or not careful as listeners. You let the Word down.

Remember Paul's admonition: "Think on these things." A seed does not produce its potentialities in a moment. Its principle is growth; and its process is germination. Quietness is the seed's growing place; meditation is the mood for the seed's unfolding; thought is the sphere for the seed's action.

• • •

Certain suggestive and helpful insights are gained by understanding the nature and task of Confession in relation to the nature of the Word. Confession is an individual's response, in a church, to the leading of the Word. If the Word of God is understood as the Lord's incessant salvatory activity of love and judgment operative in history, then the act of confession (with a small c) is immediately seen in a double aspect. A confession is both then and now. It is a hallowed historical monument that serves to direct, protect against vagaries and idiosyncratic distortions, and insure that basic issues of the religious life remain basic. The Word of God is a *given*; it is also a *giving*, by which the given is animated into contemporary address. It is an endowment of revelation in Scripture; it is also a contemporary activity of God whereby the Scriptures are transmitted fresh and new for each generation's need.

• • •

The Word of God always dwells among us as both grace and judgment. And the judgments in our time may be more eloquent than the appearance of the grace. When one looks at the awesome history of the twentieth century, with its murderous wars and the decline in what we used to call the piety of the Christian community, one begins to see that the judgment of God is at work in the failure of our successes, in the negative results that follow upon what we believe to be completely positive actions. When the things on which we have rested our hopes turn out to be incapable of delivering the goods we had hoped for, this is grace by way of judgment; it is education by way of disappointment, and illumination by way of darkness. In the Old Testament, God led the people home by way of the wilderness. That may not be the most comfortable way to go home, but it may sometimes be the only way.

A Profession of Faith

I believe the Christian faith because I know of no other story which in its tragedy and its pathos, its joy and its delight, has expressed life both in its disorganized and its organized activity with anything like the veracity, the vivacity, the actuality, and the ductility to all human life that characterize this story.

Preaching at Yale

I got into the pulpit and, with no introduction, asked, "What's going on here?" The text in question was the parable of the unjust steward, which I proceeded to take apart, trying to analyze its dynamics. Coming to the climactic point, I said, "And the Lord commended this crook." I got all the dynamics and asked: "What is in this man who is manifestly a crook? The Lord does not commend his morality—he has nothing to do with that. But there is that in the man's action which our Lord found commendable." I simply let it hang there—and then pronounced "Amen."

There is (or was, anyway) an interesting custom at Yale: students and others retire to a coffee shop after a service to sit around and talk about the sermon or jaw with the preacher. Someone is always assigned to open the discussion; he or she is critic for the day. In this case, it was George Lindbeck—now that's hard on any preacher. George leaned back and said: "Well, I didn't hear a sermon today. The preacher really didn't advise me on what I ought to think or help me along the way as to how I ought to behave and act and what things I ought to attend to. I didn't hear a sermon. I don't really know what he was up to. He just told me a story and said, 'Amen.'"

There was a deadly silence; perhaps the students were thinking, "George, you can't be so rough on a guest." Finally the silence was broken by a girl in the corner who stood up and announced: "He did too say something. I don't know what he said, but I can't forget that crazy question." And George, in his mild way, stopped smoking his pipe long enough to comment, "Maybe that's what he's up to; I don't know."

Unshriveled Sensibilities

There is such a thing as a Christian culture that evaluates the godless beauties of humankind more highly than the godless teachers do. In other words, when I speak to the university, I try to speak in such a way as to show that my humanistic sensibilities are not shriveled by virtue of my being a Christian. And that is often a shock to my listeners.

Preaching to a Cliché

Many in this generation have the highly individual sense that "the world is such a mess that I'm going to have to do things my own way and figure them out in my own way and make what I can of my own life." I understand that sentiment. But in preaching to this generation—for instance in university chapels—I have tried often to preach self-consciously and openly to one of these clichés that I hear all over the place, for instance, the one that says, "I want to be on top of the world." Well, you know, that is no place from which to relate oneself to the world—on top of it. One ought to be inside of it, or part of it, or even sometimes under it. But "on top of it"—that's a phony idea.

I once preached a sermon which I am glad was not tape-recorded because it was almost pornographic. I took a sentence from the Song of Songs and the young audience thought, "Boy, this guy (not only the guy who wrote the Song of Songs but the preacher for the morning) really understands us." I included a number of delicious parts from Donne and Shakespeare to build up the rhetoric of sensuality and so forth. And then the last five minutes of the sermon were: "But don't kid yourself. Why is it that some of the deepest literature in every language points to the tristesse d'amour, the sadness that occurs after the act of love? Now that is psychologically true; there is a kind of sadness. What does that sadness mean but that many things are good and delightful, but they are not God, they are not absolute? 'Thou hast formed us for thyself, O Lord, and our hearts are restless till we rest in thee.' Copulation is a great idea, but it is not absolutely fulfilling of humanity. So I do not want you to build yourself up for an absolute letdown. Amen."

In a sense you can say the last things because you have talked so provocatively about the first thing; they know you know what you are talking about. Therefore they will listen to the end of the sermon because you have established your credentials in the first part.

The Language of Worship

Language in our time has become flat, nonallusive, and impoverished. What might this situation mean for our churches as they seek to recover ways of worship that will be more fully reflective of the long history of the people of God in their life of worship?

It is strange that this problem, so widely acknowledged and so profoundly disturbing outside the churches, has, so far as I know, not been systematically discussed among us. This is the more strange because the more deeply a concern is loaded with history, the past, and things accomplished long ago, the more a church understands itself as a "pilgrim people of God"—that is, called, continuous, on the way, starting with a constitutive deed and living out its life in a hope that is both a given and an awaited consummation. The more clearly the church understands *that*, the more embarrassing its problem with a flat and impoverished language. Just as our Christology becomes richer, our ecclesiology more organic, our anthropology deeper—our common language, the cultural instrument that must do the work of acknowledgment, praise, and interpretation, is shrinking in obedience to a diminished realm of meaning.

The gravity of rhythmic speech is the mark of a culture that carries its past livingly in its present experience. Rhythmic speech is the outward and visible sign of rootedness. Every society has had its rhetoric of remembrance. "Come now, let us bring our reasoning to a close, saith the Lord. . . . Israel doth not know, my people doth not consider. . . . I am the Lord thy God that brought thee out of that great and terrible wilderness. . . . I have called thee by thy name, thou art mine."

In the Scriptures, each moment is heavy with all past moments; for the God of the moment is the Creator of the continuity. The old prayers of the church understood this so well and felt it so deeply that every one of them jumps into the moment's petitions after a running start in the eventful history of the people of God. "O God, who didst teach the hearts of Thy faithful people by sending to them the light of Thy Holy Spirit: Grant us by the same Spirit to have a right judgment in all things, and evermore to rejoice in His holy comfort . . ." This is great rhetoric because it roots the life of the moment in the grace of the past; it evokes a response in depth because it is not only a report, but a reverberation. It is an expectant episode in a people's life because it is a note in ancient and continuing music. It is as big as the heart because it is as old as the people of God.

How many times, in reading the liturgy for the Holy Communion, I have felt both exultation and despair at the moment of the Sanctus: "Therefore with Angels and Archangels, and with all the company of heaven, we laud and magnify Thy glorious Name; evermore praising Thee and saying: Holy, Holy, Holy, Lord God of Sabaoth . . ." Exalted because in this language this place and time and company of momentary lives are interpreted and blessed within the scope of an eternal action of God, released from the tyranny of death and what Dylan Thomas has so movingly alluded to when he laments that

time allows
In all his tuneful turning so few and such morning songs . . .*

But also in despair, for to the flattened speech of our time angels and archangels are rather ridiculous symbols—material, so to speak, nonfissionable by contemporary definition of fact.

Strange things, nevertheless, are happening in the present practice of language. Just when one is sodden with despair over

---

* Dylan Thomas, "Fern Hill," *The Collected Poems of Dylan Thomas* (New York: New Directions, 1964), p. 179. Copyright 1946 by New Directions Publishing Corporation. Copyright 1952 by Dylan Thomas. Reprinted by permission of New Directions Publishing Corporation.

the possibility of making alive the massive biblical symbol of fire—for instance,

> Come Holy Ghost, our souls inspire
> And lighten with celestial fire—

just then humanity does such things with language as to reinvest this symbol with meanings, and dreamed-of meanings, of terrible force. The immediate referent of *fire* is not the celestial fire of God's descending and recreating ardor, but a monstrous shape like a death-dealing mushroom. And out of this unimaginable hell a man envisions again an unbelievable grace, and writes in language which wildly fuses destroying atom bombs and the descending Holy Ghost.

> The dove descending breaks the air
> With flame of incandescent terror
> Of which the tongues declare
> The one discharge from sin and error
> The only hope, or else despair
>   Lies in the choice of pyre or pyre—
>   To be redeemed from fire by fire.
>
> Who then devised the torment? Love.
> Love is the unfamiliar Name
> Behind the hands that wove
> The intolerable shirt of flame
> Which human power cannot remove.
>   We only live, only suspire
>   Consumed by either fire or fire.*

Such speech judges one's tepid unbelief in the power of the Holy Spirit of God, reminds us that the aggressive and ingenious love that can make the stones cry out can penetrate positivistic language too and betimes torment its flatness into a kind of "negative" praise.

* From "Little Gidding" in *Four Quartets* by T. S. Eliot, copyright 1943 by T. S. Eliot; renewed 1971 by Esme Valerie Eliot. Reprinted by permission of Harcourt Brace Jovanovich, Inc.

Nobody Wants Barabbas

In order to gain the real meaning in the Gospel story of the man Barabbas we must not accent the choice of Barabbas, but the rejection of Jesus. The tragedy is deeper and more subtle than appears on the surface. In a real sense the people did not choose Barabbas. The man had put himself outside the community of Israel by his detestable deeds. That this man should have been restored in the affections of his people even after this day is inconceivable. But the man is freed! The people had determined to reject Jesus; and Barabbas was the alternative. The rejection was the decision. They didn't really say yes to Barabbas; but they did say no to Jesus. Barabbas was all that was left.

This event is but a dramatic condensation of something Jesus had been saying all along: decision is a tough but necessary business in life, and in the relationship of humanity with God there is no middle ground. "Ye cannot serve God and mammon!" Not ought not. *Cannot!* Most of us nevertheless think we can. We use mammon, support our lives upon the stuff of mammon. And then after a time, the rewards and advantages of mammon grow and grow—and we find ourselves able and willing to love, serve, and obey it.

The whole matter of choice was central to Jesus' preaching. When he said, "Who is not for me, who gathereth not with me scattereth," he made a complex fact about human life very plain—and painful. As before the announcement of the Kingdom of God, there is no neutrality, there are no sidelines, and there are no noncombatants. To fail to choose, or to refuse to choose, does not mean that choice is thereby avoided. To refuse to choose is already to choose *to refuse to choose!*

This event relates to a fatal disposition in our modern culture. It's a culture that wants to avoid decision, choice, all the uncultivated harshness of the either/or. We incline to believe that there is a certain structure, momentum, direction in life and that by virtue of inherent harmonies working out their admittedly troubled music, everything will come out all right. Democracy for instance. It is a noble idea, and a sound doctrine for the ordering of human existence. But it didn't get established and working because the idea was symmetrical or the doctrine plausible. It was willed into existence by choice, resolution, the dedicated lives of intent people with set jaws. And it can't be maintained without the exercise of those choices that gave it birth and life. It must be steadily willed, vigorously applied, constantly criticized, loyally sacrificed for.

And family. Family is wide open to forces that sometimes quickly smash. Family too must be willed—by a resolute stance taken against everything that would weaken and finally destroy it.

But to mobilize and get the will a-marching is hard work. We haven't much time for what that work requires: the long, deep look and the stout stand.

When Jesus talked of a saving narrowness, of loyal repudiations and loyal assertions, of a breadth born of cauterizing narrowness and a joy granted to a suffering will, he was beating out a single grand theme: desires without decisions are disastrous. Our desires are infinite. The streetcar named Desire is copious, and it jogs along forever. But finally it won't create an eternal life out of these bundles of casual or passionate experience who ride it.

There is a quick sort of terror in the story of Barabbas. Nobody wants Barabbas. But the man is on the loose and on our hands.

46

The View from Mount Nebo

And Moses went up from the plains of Moab to Mount Nebo, to the top of Pisgah, which is opposite Jericho. And the Lord showed him all the land, Gilead as far as Dan, all Naphtali, the land of Ephraim and Manasseh, all the land of Judah as far as the Western Sea, the Negeb, and the Plain, that is, the valley of Jericho the city of palm trees, as far as Zoar. And the Lord said to him, "This is the land of which I swore to Abraham, to Isaac, and to Jacob, 'I will give it to your descendants.' I have let you see it with your eyes, but you shall not go over there." So Moses the servant of the Lord died there in the land of Moab, according to the word of the Lord, and he buried him in the valley in the land of Moab opposite Bethpeor; but no man knows the place of his burial to this day. Moses was a hundred and twenty years old when he died; his eye was not dim, nor his natural force abated. And the people of Israel wept for Moses in the plains of Moab thirty days; then the days of weeping and mourning for Moses were ended.

And Joshua the son of Nun was full of the spirit of wisdom, for Moses had laid his hands upon him; so the people Israel obeyed him, and did as the Lord had commanded Moses. And there has not arisen a prophet since in Israel like Moses, whom the Lord knew face to face, none like him for all the signs and the wonders which the Lord sent him to do in the land of Egypt, to Pharaoh and to all his servants and to all his land, and for all the mighty power and all the great and terrible deeds which Moses wrought in the sight of all Israel.   (Deuteronomy 34)

One should not oversimplify the Christian doctrine of the Holy Spirit. That doctrine declares that faith is a work of God's Spirit, that it is God alone who can cause an individual in full personal decision to make the Christian confession.

But sometimes we so speak, or more often sing, of the work of the Holy Spirit as to reduce to a single and simple way the enormous variety of ways the Holy Spirit accomplishes his work. One such oversimplification is celebrated in the hymn that has a melancholy popularity among many young people's groups:

47

Blessed assurance, Jesus is mine.
Oh, what a foretaste of glory divine.

What this hymn suggests is that nothing Christian is authentic until and unless it has become a blessed assurance in some specifiable, warm, pervasive, and crucial experience.

This assumption points to a truth—and it encourages an error. The truth is that a person is an organic whole and that there is a continuity between outside and inside, appearance and reality. There is a momentum between confession and total being. But the error is the assumption that Christian faith is normally identical with what has been confirmed in that way. This assumption is not only erroneous, it is dangerous. For it invites the mind to reduce the Christian pronouncement and claim to those elements which have been certified in the heat of one's individual experience. Such an error is both reductive and distorting, for it shrinks and twists the magnificence, the scope, and the objectivity of Christian fact to the dimension of personal and largely temperamental endowments. It tempts us to hang the reality of God, the compass of his demands, the scope of biblical and theological meaning upon a febrile nail: the warmth and immediacy of a feeling of blessed assurance.

This subjectivizing of the Christian faith presents problems for us. Instead of speaking of these abstractly I will speak of one such problem as I know it concretely. For some years I was dean of students in a theological seminary of my church and had frequently to talk with students who came to me disturbed because their sense of vocation was not as strong, or as inwardly certified, as they felt it ought to be if they were going to be ordained ministers of the Christian gospel. They said, "I believe the gospel and that a person ought to preach it. But how do I know that this task is for me? I don't have that interior confirmation whereby I feel a sense of absolute certainty in my vocation as a Christian minister."

I have sometimes been able to be of help to such students

because I have walked and continue to walk that same tightrope. I feel the same absence of this "blessed assurance" in my own life. I too make uncertified postulation of the Christian faith, uncertified, that is, by auxiliary feelings that are supposed somehow to make it "more true." In my experience in teaching and preaching the story of the Christian faith I recall an instance in my own parish when I was preaching straight through Philippians. I did pretty well through the first part of the first chapter. This part is historical and reportorial; I could simply say that this is what happened to Paul, and this is the way he responded. Then I came to the verse that really gets down to the nitty-gritty, verse 21 in the first chapter: "For to me to live is Christ, and to die is gain." I had to begin my sermon by saying, "I must declare to you something this morning that I do not know anything about." My job was not to say, "This is true, and I can testify that it is true," because I would have been a liar to say that. I had not yet come to the point (and I still have not yet come to it) where I can say, "If I die today it is all right with me. For me to die is gain." I do not have the gifts of grace whereby I can say this. My duty, instead, is to say that the man who said the other true things in the first chapter of Philippians did not suddenly turn into a phony when he said this! "I don't know that this is so, but Saint Paul knew that it was so" was a proper statement. My duty was to say that grace has this magnificent possibility, it *can* do that to a person, and for Paul, it did. He could then say that "if they take me to Rome and cut my head off next week or whether I return to you at Philippi is no longer the fundamental issue."

I wish I had so rich and gallant a gift. But my duty is not to reduce the message to the size of what I have or have not; it is proper sometimes to declare what one does not know.

But is this just my problem? Is it just my pilgrimage? I think not. There are thousands of students today to whom the Christian faith must be declared as if they too stood in that same position. And it is for this reason that I have chosen the title "The View from Mount Nebo." It suggests different perspectives for looking in upon things. There are many mountains in the Bible: Mount Hermon, Mount Zion, Mount Calvary. But there is that other peak, Mount Nebo. And I ask you to regard this peak as a kind of symbol by which to elucidate a way of standing within the problem of "blessed assurance."

Think of three perspectives from which one can envision and begin to talk about the Christian faith. First, the perspective from within. Most talk about Christianity does, and should, proceed from this warm, immediate perspective from within the body of the people of God in Christ. They speak out of and in the language of this beloved community which knows what it means to have been redeemed from the insecurities and egocentricities of perilous life. They are firmly held by the action of God, speak of it with adoration, understanding, enthusiasm. The great objective story of Christianity has been reenacted within their own experience in such a way that an outer nativity at Bethlehem has become an inner nativity whereby they know a new birth. An incarnation *there* has wrought a strange new person *here*. A death in the great story is now interpreted to be a death of self from which one rises in answer to the outer resurrection to a newness of life in every moment of one's breathing existence. This perspective from within, which I see and partly understand, is always the first central perspective for declaring the Christian story. Christ is love, and joy, peace, hope; and all these gifts are given by the Holy Ghost. They are, as Paul says, "the fruits of the Spirit."

It is only honest to say that I have never known fully that kind of life within the full, warm power of that faith for whose declaration I am an ordained minister. The very term "Christian experience," as generally understood, has small meaning for me. I have not seen any burning bushes. I have not pounded at the door of God's grace with the passion of a Martin Luther.

John Wesley's "strangely warmed" heart at Aldersgate Street—this is not my street. I have not the possibility to say of the Christian faith what many honest persons have said about it. But I have come to see that to declare as a gift of God that which I do not fully possess is, nevertheless, a duty of obedience. Is the opulence of the grace of God to be measured by my inventory? Is the great catholic faith of nineteen centuries to be reduced to my interior dimensions? Are the arching lines of the gracious "possible" to be pulled down to the little spurts of my personal compass? Is the great heart of the reality of God to speak in only the broken accent that I can follow after? No. That ought not to be. Therefore, one is proper and right to sometimes talk of things one doesn't know all about. In obedience to the bigness of the story which transcends personal apprehension, one may do this.

A second perspective is the one from without. The first perspective is characterized by participation, the second by detachment. The view from without has not the same legitimacy or the same kind of power as the view from within. But it has, nevertheless, its own power, its own function, and it addresses students of today with a particular kind of velocity. It is primarily critical, reportorial, or, as the student in sciences would call it, phenomenological. It asks what it means to be a Christian. What does this community called Christian intend, whence did it come, what did it affirm as it came into history, how is this community constituted, what does it declare about the nature of truth and reality, how has it embodied its affirmations in cultural-historical institutions and in ethics?

Now asking these questions is perhaps not a very exciting way to be a Christian. But I should like to suggest that you think of what the Christian community owes to the quiet persons who view from this second perspective. These are persons who never raise their voices in declaration or declamation, seldom give praise in public, never offer moving testimonials. Who knows what goes on in the hearts of people who lack the grace of adoration, of passion, of immediate "blessed assurance," who lack full knowledge of God, who must live out their lives in hard, dutiful obedience to lesser, cooler graces because their lives are unattended by the hotter ones? The lives of such Christians are given, rather, to discernment, critical work, the effort to achieve a precise description of what is really involved in becoming and being a Christian.

I once studied for some months in a German university. One of my professors was a great teacher of preaching. This man could not preach, and he never tried to. He was too honest to claim to have what the Bible talks about and promises. But he knew what the biblical promise was, he knew that when the Bible talks of the Kingdom of God it does not mean habitual piety, puritan mores, better homes and gardens, middle-class respectability, soul sweetness and body cleanliness, inoffensive community acceptability. He knew that when he was talking about redemption, salvation, sin, faith, or grace, he was talking about huge and clear realities. He would not permit us to palm off phony realities in the name of these. He knew that whether he had the gift of these realities or not, they do constitute what it means to be a Christian.

The third perspective is the one shared by many of us who are students. It has a peculiar pathos, a peculiar toughness, honesty, and promise for the days that lie ahead. It is the perspective of many today who do not know if they ought to call themselves Christians at all, but who are saddened in their feeling of being outside the Christian company.

It is this third perspective which is suggested by the passage from Deuteronomy concerning Moses on Mount Nebo. Recall what you know about Moses. This man was a strong, spiritual, and faithful man.

Moses was a strong man. He steadfastly pointed with all the force of his massive personal power to the will of God for his people. He kept their ears open to God, he kept their faces turned toward their destiny, and he kicked their reluctant feet along the road to their heavenly possession. Michelangelo's great actualization of the figure of Moses is not wrong: that awesome figure is all the trouble and the Exodus and the hard wilderness of Israel portrayed in stone.

Moses was a spiritual man. He was determined by the Spirit that called him to live his life under a certain discipline and task. Spiritual does not mean to be wrapped in a kind of holy gas which becomes ignited around testimonial campfires. For Moses it meant to have his will and decisions determined by the Spirit of God. He knew that God had a will for his people and that the human spirit was to be subjected to that great Spirit. He was, therefore, a lawgiver, that is, the voice of the Spirit of God who constituted this particular people and gave them particular laws. Moses would never let them forget that—and Deuteronomy is his monument.

Moses was a faithful man. He obeyed even when he did not understand. He held to the command. He obeyed the vision in Egypt, in the wilderness, on Mount Sinai, and even on Mount Nebo.

Moses on Mount Nebo was in the situation of many of us who feel we must confess and serve a faith whose gifts to us are not given with all the opulence we might desire, and in whose lives the very gifts of grace do not control us who are the declarers of these same gifts. Here is a perspective from which many persons must view the life of the church, the tradition, and the pathos of one's own position. Moses saw clearly, but he could not enter into what he saw. The poorest child of that people who entered into the land of promise had what Moses, who led them to the land, could never have. Moses had sight without actuality; he had knowledge without possession. Moses knew more about what Israel meant than did most people ever to be in Israel. But he died outside the land.

53

At this particular moment in our religion and intellectual history, the perspective from Mount Nebo is a necessary one. It is good for many of today's college students to see the man who from Nebo's peak was yet strong, spiritual, faithful. For students are being invited to sit in the cozy rooms of religious togetherness and seek violently after "commitment"—a kind of contemporary term for the older blessed assurance. And many of them can't bring it off. The conventional standard psychological equipment of blessed assurance has not been given them. They are critical, historically self-conscious, they know a thing or two about the vast variety of stages on the way to the Christian confession, and they are not disposed to indulge in too-quick oversimplifications.

It is at such a moment that the perspective from Mount Nebo may be useful to us. The people of Mount Nebo are the obedient children of both participation and detachment. They know and they do not know fully. They participate because they come from the tradition and tuition of the faith, and have been so deeply formed by it that they cannot escape its terms, its claims, its ethics. And they do not want to. They know the power and the good of the God-relationship in all things: they know it to be true, and rich, and free. They want to be open to the renewing power of the Holy, but at the same time, while they participate, they do not fully enter. Their participation is a kind of "hurt" participation: they do not possess those gifts of the Spirit—love, joy, peace, hope—which would permit them without a kind of sardonic footnote to sing, "Blessed assurance, Jesus is mine." Nevertheless, they want to affirm those very gifts as being a possibility of God for the world.

Now from the inside, for many of us tormented by this precise perspective, this means that we must sometimes envision with the mind what the heart cannot yet confirm, must see and affirm with clear intellectual sight what we have not been given the grace to celebrate in actual life. And yet, how great is our debt to those *without* grace who out of the passion of their poverty sing the songs of grace!

Think, for instance, of Sören Kierkegaard, that great Christian man, who out of a loveless love wrote of love with excruciating penetration. Just as the hungry talk of food, or the thirsty of water, so does this mordant man who loved hopelessly write of human love with a penetration and a passion which few have ever equaled. Here is a strange fact: precision in knowledge and statement may have two mothers, and they are in contradiction. There is a precision that is born of knowledge: the clear, joyous precision of the insider who lives completely with the faith. St. Francis had it. John Calvin had it. And there is the other precision: the precision begotten of deprivation, the tormented precision of vision without gift. There are persons in the Christian tradition who have described the reality of certain graces because they lived their lives, not within the vitality and fragrance of these graces, but because they stood outside longingly looking in and described with tormented precision what they saw. These are the ones of Mount Nebo who see what their feet cannot touch, and out of negation forge those clear descriptions which then become the dear possession of the children of the land. These are the ones who in sheer thought forge ideas in longing that others affirm in quiet and unquestioning possession. Pathos gives a toughness that affirmation profits by.

Now, you will tell me, faith without works is dead, and you are quite right. The people of Mount Nebo know this with an excruciating clarity that the calm quoters of the passage seldom know. And out of their poverty they fashion the only possible gift they can bring to the faith—a clarity given to the bereft that enables others to know and to find.

On the peak of Nebo, between participation without substance and detachment without peace, they add their astringent voice to the song of faith. Without the lean ones of Nebo, the people on Mount Zion are always tempted to become fat. There is a beatitude in the New Testament that reads, "Blessed are they that hunger and thirst, . . . for they shall be filled." I would suggest to this disconsolate student generation that in the long history of the intellectual life of the church, and having a poignant force in these confusing days when the very nature of Christian truth and its relation to the world is being refashioned, a second little beatitude may be wrought out for our comfort in a lesser and a stranger way: "Blessed also are they that hunger and thirst without being filled." For just to hunger and thirst, and to knowing without settling for it that you *do* hunger and thirst, is given a kind of negative benediction. Hunger, unabated, is a kind of testimony to the reality of food. To want to have may become a strange kind of having.

Maceration of the Minister

The church says that it wants better preaching—and really means it. But there is in this demand some bitter irony for the preacher. To preach well requires time, reflection, solitude; and the church makes other demands of the preacher that annihilate these three requirements. The situation I propose to describe is already and painfully well-known to the clergy, and if an address to them has only an intermural value, they are perhaps comforted in their pain by the knowledge that others know of it.

It is nevertheless said here on the purely tactical ground that someone ought to speak out against what I call the maceration of the minister. Someone ought to do so with plain, reportorial force—not as a psychologist, internist, or time-study expert, but as a churchperson within the context of a convocation traditionally concerned with the practical well-being of the churches.

I sought for a less violent term to designate what I behold, but maceration was the only one sufficiently accurate. Among the meanings of the term listed in the dictionary is this grim one: *to chop up into small pieces.* That this is happening to thousands of ministers does not have to be argued or established; it needs only to be aggressively stated. The minister's time, focused sense of vocation, vision of his or her central task, mental life, and contemplative acreage—these are all under the chopper. Observation leads me to conclude, too, that this fact is general. The person who looks back thirty years to ordination is in no better circumstance than the one who looks back three years. The one who is minister in an established parish and surrounded with a staff has substantially the same complaint as the mission minister with a self-propelled mimeograph. Nor does the church body in which the person is a minister, or the distinction or obscurity of the school which awarded a degree in divinity, make any perceivable difference.

What the schools elevate the actual practice of the ministry flattens. The schools urge to competence in the various fields of theological study. The canons of competence that determine the churches' practice are not only strange to what the schools supply and encourage, they are radically destructive of their precedence and nurture. There is something positively sardonic in a quick jump from a remembered student in a remembered classroom to the pastor in the parish. I have done many such jumps and the effect is disheartening. In the classroom the student was told that the *basileia tou theou,* for instance, is a phrase of enormous scope and depth, and that the declaration of it should be informed by such studies as were taught in class. It was further urged that such study ought to persist throughout life. The teachers were concerned that the student not become so insensible as to make such easy identifications with the Kingdom of God as characterize the promotional theological literature of our burgeoning churches.

Visit the former student some years later in what he or she calls inexactly the "study," and one is more than likely to find the pastor accompanied by volumes taken from the student room. Filed on top of these will be mementos of present concerns: a roll of blueprints; a file of negotiations between the parish, the bank, and the Board of Missions; samples of asphalt tile; and a plumber's estimate.

When one wonders what holds this pastor together, what allows equal enthusiasm for practical decisions and pastoral and proclamatory function, one learns that if he or she is held together at all, it is by the public role of responsibility for the external advancement of the congregation. The terms in which this advancement are commonly assessed seep backward and downward to transform the pastor's interior relation to his or her studies. Those studies become less and less an occupation engaged in for the clarification of the role as witness to the gospel and pastor to people, and become more and more frantic efforts to find biblical or theological generalities that will religiously dignify the minister's promotional purposes. The will of God has got to be simplified into a push for the parish house. The Holy Spirit is reduced to a holy resource that can be used as a punch line for the enforcement of parish purposes. The theme of Christian obedience must be stripped of its judging ambiguities and forthwith used as a lever to secure commitment that is somehow necessarily correlated with observable services to the current and clamant program. The message, in short, is managed in terms of its instrumental usefulness for immediate goals. "Arise, and let us go hence" becomes a text so epigrammatically apt that it were a shame to lose it by the complication of context or exegesis.

Where are the originating places of this process, and what forms does it take? There are, I think, three that are so obvious and constant that they can be named and described. But even these are to be recognized as functions of a force that is pervasive and underlies them all. This basic force is a loss of the sense of the particularity of the church, the consequent transformation of the role of the minister into that of a "religious leader," and the still-consequent shift whereby the ministry is regarded as a "profession," and theological education has come to understand its task as "professional education." Had this shift in meanings not occurred, the three specific forces I am about to name could hardly have been effective. But the shift has occurred—and the minister is macerated by pressures emanating from the parish, the general church bodies, and the "self-image of the minister."

The Parish: The very vocabulary that has become common is eloquent. The parish has a "plant," its nature or purpose is specified in terms of a "program" for which a "staff" is responsible to a "board." The "program" is evaluated in terms of palpable production which can be totaled with the same hard-boiled facticity as characterizes a merchandising operation—and commonly is. The minister, like it or not, is the executive officer. I know of a synod of a church body which, wishing to put the matter of financial support of the "program" of the church on a less obviously allocated basis than characterizes the property tax office of the municipality, came up with a "fresh" idea: each member should give as the Lord had prospered that person. The synod called it the "grace *system*"!

This systematization of the holy betrays, if nothing worse, a peculiar atrophy of a Protestant sense of humor. Our theology of stewardship is pragmatically translated into terms and operational devices which deny the theology we affirm. The path to such practices is easily discernible. After a generation or two during which paid quartets, in the better-heeled parishes, weekly praised God as surrogates for the congregation, and professional organizations raised the money for "plant expansion" (all, of course, with a well-oiled unction that would have glazed the eyeballs of St. Paul), it is not surprising that the counsel to stewardship should be preceded, according to some church programs, by an inquisitorial scrutiny of the share of each of the sheep in the gross national product. The reply, of course, is that it works. There can be no doubt that it does. The same reply, however, if made normative for the truth of the entire nature and scope of the meaning of the church, would indicate that the theology of prayer ought to take account of the reported correlation between petition and the growth rate of potted plants.

The Christian community always walks close to the edge of superstition, magic, and the strange human desire to translate grace into a workable lubricant for the parish. There is a relation between an immeasurable gift of grace and the responding gifts of humanity to advance the institutional celebration of the gospel of grace. But it is the task of theology, as it ought to be a concern of planned parish preaching and instruction, to witness to this grace in such a way as to raise Christian eyebrows over every perverting proposal to mechanize it.

There is no evidence that policy deters perversion. A church in a surplice is as easily seduced as a church in a black robe, or one with neither of these. That the "business of America is business" has bequeathed to us all a vocabulary, a point of view, canons of evaluation that are so deeply rooted in our parishes that perhaps nothing short of a Kierkegaardian attack upon Christendom will suffice for renovation.

The General Church Bodies: What characterizes the mind of the parish is but amplified, solidified, and given enhanced authority in the larger world of the general bodies. Some years ago it became apparent to certain large corporations that they had succeeded so well in fashioning the company men into symmetrical functionaries that a danger was recognized. A few eccentrics were deliberately sought out, protected, and asked to give themselves to reflection uninhibited by charts.

Such sardonic maturity has not yet arisen within the churches. The fantastic rigidity, the almost awesome addiction to "channels," the specialization of concern and operation that characterize our structure have made us, in large part, prisoners of accredited mediocrity. "The wind bloweth where it listeth," but when it does, a shudder of embarrassment racks the structure from top to bottom. If another J. S. Bach should appear in my church and succeed, as the first one did, in giving a new deep piety a new and adequate voice, he would have to plead his case before elected or appointed arbiters whose authority exceeds that of the consistory of Köthen or Leipzig—and whose general cultivation is less.

The informing and edifying of the church through charismatic endowments by the Holy Spirit is not incompatible with the doctrine of the one holy catholic and apostolic church. But it is incompatible with the church order that takes its model from the more banal children of this world. We affirm the charismatic in piety and imprison it in established structures in practice. It has actually come to pass that our churches maintain a disciplined cadre of inspirational operators. These persons are on call for whatever program the church from time to time decides to accent. They can blow any horn one hands them. If the program involves support for educational institutions, they stand ready to declare across the broad reaches of the land in districts, conferences, and parishes that "the future of the church hangs upon the success of the venture in education." And when at the next general convention the scene shifts to rural missions, the same enthusiasm, now supplied with a changed terminology and directed toward a changed goal, is sent out on the road from general headquarters. One has heard this interchangeable vivacity vocalize so many and such various projects as to be reminded that the salesman is a category that can be defined quite independently of the product sold. Whether his sample case contains hammer handles or lingerie is nothing to the point.

The Self-image of the Minister: The transformation of the minister's self-image is the third force contributing to the maceration. The effects of this transformation at the deepest levels of the individual's personal life can hardly be spoken of in terms that are too grave. For this image is, strictly, not a professional or merely personal or even church-official image. It is rather an image given with the office of the ministry in and by a church in obedience to the command of the Lord of the gospel. The "ministry of the Word and Sacraments" belongs to no person; all believers belong to it. And among these some are acknowledged as having been given a charism, undergone preparation, and announced their intention to serve the gospel in this particular ministry. In the full gravity of this gift, task, and intention, a person is ordained to this ministry, charged in specific terms drawn from the dominical imperative faithfully to fulfill it. The self-image of the minister is then more than a self-image; it is an image of the vocation and task of the self gathered up into a gift and a task that was before the self came to be, having a reality that transcends while it involves the whole self, and which will be bestowed upon the church by the Lord when this particular self is no longer of the church in history.

Fragmentation has become a common term in psychology and sociology. But what has happened to the ministry is all that term suggests and reports, but more painful and accusatory because of the gravity of that public bestowing and receiving of the Lord's ministry of Word and Sacrament. A vase can be fragmented; maceration is what a human being feels when fragmented.

It is difficult for the minister to maintain a clear vision of the self when so seldom doing what he or she ought. The self-image of a servant of the gospel has been slowly clarified, carefully matured, informed, and sensitized during years of preparation. At the time of ordination, the church publicly and thankfully acknowledged a gift, a discipline, and a person's intention to assume a task.

All of this is under constant attrition in the present form of the churches. And thus it comes about that honesty in the fulfillment of the minister's central task is gradually laid aside in favor of sincerity. *Sincerity* is a term a person uses to enable the self to live with itself in the face of uneasy questions about honesty. There remain, however, deep down but insistent, voices and remembrances that tell the person what is going on and that the exchange is not a good one. And the enthusiastic readiness of parish and church to accept, even to applaud, the shift makes the suffering of the minister the more acute.

There have been a number of studies, some widely publicized, in which attention has been called to the large number of crack-ups of various degrees of severity among the clergy. The supporting testimony is impressive. The reasons most often suggested are too much work, too long a day, too various a complex of problems and duties, too unremitting a drain on emotional and mental stores, insufficient opportunity to lift the clerical nose from the parish grindstone.

While these facts are present and powerful, the sum of them does not, I think, get to the heart of the matter. They are too obvious, too shallow; they do not designate what comes out—stumbling, embarrassed, and often gestured rather than stated—when one observes and listens with attention. From many hours spent with many former students I have learned that there is a constant fact in the variety of their confessions, overt or oblique.

These persons are deeply disturbed because they have a sense of vocational guilt. This guilt is so strong, so clear, and so deeply sunk in their central self-consciousness that one knows with an immediate impatience that no diminution of hours or other rearrangements of outer life can have decisive effect.

This sense of guilt has an observable content. A minister has been ordained to an Office, but too often ends up running an office. Solemnly ordained to the ministry in Christ's church, most of the pastors I know really want to be what they intended and prepared for. Instead they have ended up in a kind of dizzy occupational oscillation. They are aware of the truth of what Karl Barth said in one of his earliest addresses: "Our people expect us to take them more seriously than they take themselves, and they will not thank us if we do not do so." Most ministers are aware that it is a tough and delicate labor to insert the lively power of the Word of God into the rushing occupations and silent monologues of human beings. Most recall with a sense of joy the occasions when honest work and unhurried reflection gave a strange victory to their efforts. But these occasions are infrequent, set amid great stretches of guilt-begetting busyness.

What, then, is to be done? From each of the designated constituents of the problem a different response is required. There are the professors in schools of theology, the parishes, the officials in the general bodies, the ministers themselves. Upon professors in the schools of theology there rests an immediate and pressing responsibility. Our clear perception of the demolition wrought upon our labors with students, combined with the respect accorded us by our churches, urges us away from silence and toward articulate protest. We ought to be more courageous, critical, and noisy advocates for our students, more concerned protectors of their reflective future. Our intermural grousing has now the obligation to leap over the wall and seek to make itself heard among parishes and in the offices of church officialdom. For it is there that the machinery of maceration and the pounding of program are set in motion.

It is, I think, not true that the parish demands of its minister to become simply an executive officer of multiple activities. The congregation is likely to accept, support, and be deepeningly molded by the understanding of Office and calling which is projected by its minister's actual behavior. It will come to assess as central what the pastor, in the actual performance of ministry and use of time, makes central. And when this tightening and clarification of the minister's conception of the Office discloses, in the reflective depth and ordering skill of the sermon, where his or her heart and mind are centered, the parish will honor this pastoral obedience to "take them more seriously than they take themselves."

The officialdom of the church, and how it may be penetrated by a knowledge of the plight of the minister, present a more difficult—because more subtle—problem. When one beholds the staff-generated devices dreamed up by boards and commissions to focus the attention of the church-in-convention assembled upon their particular programs, one wonders if the motivation is exclusively either educational or evangelical. Have these members of promotional staffs not fallen under the sovereignty of Parkinson's Law, whereby whatever *is* tends to persist, whatever *does* is driven by dynamics strange to its purpose to do more and wider and bigger? Must not each "program" outshout the other in order to dramatize an urgency psychologically necessary for its own sense of importance, if not priority?

One does not have to operate at the top level of the ecumenical movement to suspect that the "nontheological factors" there exposed as powerful in church and theological history are operative along the whole front. It is no ingratitude toward my own family in Christendom that I take delight in the fact that there are about one hundred million of us! And the dynamics of this delight will not bear too much scrutiny in terms of the truth of the gospel, the obedience to Christ, and other such properly elevated rubrics.

We may and perhaps ought to be impatient about the world's quip that when a person becomes a bishop, that person will never thereafter eat a bad meal, read a good book, or hear the truth. But from within the family we dare a smile. For in the very generality that determines executive office, there is a power that disengages from the common table of parish existence, from the direct and pathetic book of the common life, and from the moments of sudden truth that stun and depress and exalt the minister on his or her ordinary rounds.

Finally there is the person of the minister; and in what follows I appeal to him or her from the same center as has informed this essay on preaching. The pastor, in private and imperiled existence, must fight for wholeness and depth and against erosion. By a sheer violent effort of will he or she must seek to *become* the calling, submit life and self to be shaped from the center outward. The minister need not be slapped into uncorrelated fragments of function; need not become a weary and unstructured functionary of a vague, busy moralism; need not see the visions and energies and focused loyalty of his or her calling run, shallowly like spilled water, down a multitude of slopes.

Certain practical, immediate, and quite possible steps can be taken. The temptation to improvised, catch-as-catch-can preaching, for instance, can be beaten back by calculated ordering of one's study. The most profitable period in my own parish preaching came about because I did that. What I learned in seminary about Paul of Tarsus, Paul's Christology and ethics, was not sufficient either for the great subject or for the discharge of my preaching responsibility. In one memorable year I determined to bring together concentrated study and actual preaching. Surrounding myself with the best available to me from modern Pauline scholarship, I literally lived with this man for six months, directed and taught by Adolph Deissman, James Stewart, Charles Harold Dodd, Robert Henry Lightfoot, and others.

Because the Philippian letter is the most direct, personal, and uncomplicated of Paul's letters, I resolved to preach straight through it, informing and correcting exegesis from the Greek text by the findings and insights of historians, exegetes, and theologians.

The result of this study and preaching—extending from Epiphany through Pentecost—was the establishing of a love affair with this towering and impassioned "man in Christ." I came to know him with the quick and perceptive delight one has in a friend. Paul had been fused into an adoring, obedient, proclaiming, and explicating totality by the fire of his new relation to God in "this Son of God who loved me." And the informing of all the parts of his writing by that rooted and vivacious new being in Christ, when beheld in concentrated study, opened huge new perspectives in every single verse or section. It is not necessary to add that such an exciting discipline makes quite unnecessary the weekly scrounging for a "text."

It was a sort of added dividend that when Holy Week and Easter came around, progress through the letter had landed me precisely at Philippians 2:1–11: "And being found in human form he humbled himself and became obedient unto death, even death on a cross. Therefore God has highly exalted him . . ." That section, explicated on Maundy Thursday, Good Friday, and Easter, had gained a momentum from the twelve preceding sermons on chapters 1 and 2 that was both powerful and full for the preacher and for the people.

The foregoing is an illustration, it is not a prescription. Each minister must order his or her life from the inside, and each must order it according to the requirements of interest, nature, and parish situation. But to order it is a must.

Rebellion, Repentance, and Return

Books of prophecy, books of passionate and contemplative song, books of history and chronicle—if we listen for the motif that grounds their wonderful variety, all sing out the theme of holy conflict: God-will and man-will. Not in abstract form or fictionalized persons, but richly rooted in human life and history, in nature, and in social life, the conflicts unfold the undeviating self-giving of God and the career of the Gift among us.

Old Testament history has a grand pattern; it is the weary rhythm of rebellion, repentance, and return, and over and over again the rhythm repeats itself. In the Book of Judges the writer seems actually to have managed the historical materials to accent the repetitive monotony of this pattern. Old Testament song and literature of devotion swing always and with opulent variation about the two poles: God's relentless gift of himself in steadfast love, and humanity's desperate shadow-flight from love's undismissible grounding of life. Old Testament prophecy, attached to anecdotal history at a thousand points and made articulate in many voices and many keys, has nevertheless a simple pattern. The figure of the prophet is the unsilenceable recollection of humanity's structurally given existence before God; and the upwelling voice of the prophet, through crusts of assumed independence and national self-sufficiency, through proudly contrived historical securities and subtly imagined individual safety, is the grave, recalling voice of God. The "whither shall I flee" of the individual singer has its large prophetic counterpart in the word addressed to the whole people: "I have called thee by thy name, thou art mine."

In the Old Testament drama, God's love and mercy are never presented as simply God's feeling about apostate humanity. Love and mercy are rather the forms in which God's resolute will-to-restoration presses upon humans. The love of God is a loving will, and the outstretched arm of the Eternal has many aspects. It is both a beckoning and a judging hand, but it is always there—the creator of the drama, the Holy One with whom we have inescapably to do. As the Old Testament literature moves on toward its close, the conflict tightens in both divine and mortal terms. In divine terms the assault from God tightens; hope is condensed from a holy nation to a remnant, and finally to the form of a Servant of the Lord. In mortal terms the drama of alienation depicts humanity, ingenious in evasion, flight, and self-deception, able at the last to do nothing but cry, "Oh, that thou wouldst rend the heavens, that thou wouldst come down."

Only against this background can one understand why the evangelists of the New Testament surround the nativity of Jesus Christ with heavenly messengers and choirs, poetic condensations of the hope of Israel, the Virgin's lyrical song of acceptance. Everything seems to stand still, and all things are bathed in luminous light when the new deed of God occurs in Jesus Christ. It is not in fact a strange deed if beheld from above. For God's undeviating will-to-restoration assumes there a decisive tactic of mortal involvement. But seen from below, this tactic is unique, utterly singular, for here, claim the Scriptures, is God himself, in salvatory, restorative action at the point and at the level of the original rupture. When the Fourth Gospel declares that the Word became flesh and dwelt among us, the fresh deed of God in Christ is declared in clearest terms; the involvement of the holy will can come to no closer engagement than this: "flesh," which is what I am; "among us," which is where I am.

The Living Stuff of Love

Christian ethics are inevitably christological ethics, not in the sense that such ethics are corollaries derived from propositions about Christ, but in the sense that they are faithful reenactments of that life. In the Sermon on the Mount there is revealed this obedient life in the bestowed and accepted love of God; indeed, the fulfillment and transformation of the entire Old Testament God-relationship is here revealed. As in every teaching, parable, and miracle of Jesus, there is disclosed a faith active in love which cracks all rabbinical patterns, transcends every statutory solidification of duty, breaks out of all systematic schematizations of the good—and out of the living, perceptive, restorative passion of faith enfolds in its embrace the fluctuant, incalculable, and novel emergents of human life.

Concerning the persistent desire to set forth the meaning of Christian ethics in terms of the "principles of Jesus," two things must be said. In the first place, a method in Christian ethics which works toward the achievement of clear "principles" subtly belies the very nature of the truth of Christianity. The truth of Christianity is neither abstract nor propositional; it is the truth of God incarnate in a person. "Grace and truth came by Jesus Christ." "I am the way, the truth, and the life." Truth thus acted out and bestowed in historical existence is intrinsically incapable of adequate transmission in terms of "principles." And in the second place, the desire to extrude principles from the Christ-life may be a form of our hidden human longing to make once and for all disposable, and to cool into palpable ingots of duty, the living stuff of love—and so dismiss the Holy One "with whom we have to do."

The words of the Sermon on the Mount have always been and remain an embarrassment to every effort to derive Christian ethics from Jesus according to principles of ethics. The style of

71

speech in these words of Jesus is revelatory of the ground and the living activity of the ethics of faith.

• • •

"I am crucified with Christ" is not only an expression signifying Christian recapitulation of the Christ-life in the large, but is also symbol of the inner content of numberless ethical decisions in their actual heartbreaking character. An evangelical ethics must, therefore, work where love reveals need. It must do this work in faith that comes from God and not as accumulated achievements to present to God. In this working it must seek limited objectives without apology and must support failure without despair. It can accept ambiguity without lassitude and can seek justice without identifying justice and love.

• • •

The structure of Christian ethics grows organically out of the fact and the content of the endlessly giving God. The Christian is to accept what God gives as Creator: the world with its needs, problems, and possibilities; the revelation of this world as the creature of its faithful Creator with its given orders—family, community, state, economy. Each of these is invested with the promise and potency of grace, and each of these is malleable to the perverse purposes of evil.

The Christian is to accept what God gives as Redeemer: the earth and all human life as the place wherein God's glory became flesh and dwelt among us, and therefore the holy place for life in forgiveness, in the obedience of faith, in the works of love. "Man becomes man because God became man." God has given the form of himself and his will in a man; and the ethical life is the birth pangs attending the new being of humankind in history, "until Christ be formed in you."

The Christian is to accept what God gives as Holy Spirit, the Sanctifier. This acceptance includes the gifts that God gives from above, and the tasks which he gives in the world around. These gifts and these tasks belong together. The gift is celebrated in the doing of the task; the task is undertaken in faith as witness to the gift.

Polish Sausage, St. Augustine, and the Moral Life

Every school day at twelve noon a white truck marked Hot Dogs, Polish Sausage, Coffee parks in front of the administration building at the University of Chicago. A line of persons—students, faculty, staff, white-coated medics, the buildings-and-grounds crew—begins to form and soon numbers twenty or thirty persons.

Some hot dogs are dispensed; the main item, however, is the Polish sausage sandwich. This particular sandwich is no ordinary product! Rich, juicy, odorous, garlic-laden, hot, and smelling with all the herb-subtlety of a thousand years of Polish sausage culture, this creation is lifted out of a steam-hot container, cradled in an oblong bun, and garnished with chopped onions, mustard, pickle relish, and topped with green peppers that have a shocking authority and pungency. They bring tears to the eyes, a clutch at the throat, and clarification to the mind!

The appeal of these Polish sausages is general. Less proletarian sustenance is available in several other places about the university. But the line awaiting a sausage is no respecter of prestige, learning, delicately refined tastes, professional status, or public distinction. That little man is from the art department; his job is to research Renaissance calligraphy and arrive at probable dates for Italian manuscripts. And that fellow there is doing research in low-temperature physics. The young woman in the white coat operates the electron microscope; behind her is the hard-hatted, denim-clad man who runs the pile driver at the construction job down the street. The entire congregation is lined up before the high priest in the truck; the incense is provided by the redolent magnificence of the Polish sausage.

I too used often to be in that line. One day my fellow communicant at Augustana Church was just in front of me. I was astonished to see him there—and said so: "Dr. Platz, what are you doing there? You are a pathologist; you know very well that you ought not to eat one of these violent things! They are, to be sure, among the most succulent of foods. Now I am only a theologian and don't know any better. But you are a doctor—indeed, a pathologist at that—and you have professionally examined the catastrophic effect upon the stomach of these explosive, corrosive, tissue-eroding sausages! Those fiery peppers, to mention but one component of this symphony, are enough to make the white cells cry out in anguish!"

Charles Platz fixed me with a cool gaze. "Yes," he said, "you are quite right. But these things are very good, aren't they!"

So Charles and I went on doing what we knew we shouldn't.

There you have it—the whole point of this essay: "I do not understand my own actions. I can will what is right, but I cannot do it. I do not do the good I want. . . . But the evil I do not want is what I do" (Romans 7).

St. Augustine, who knew a thing or two about the lusts of the flesh (though not, I think, very much about Polish sausage), affirmed that the human will is curved toward the good or the evil by the allure of *desire*. If the *self* is the absolute object of desire and of love, the will is curved inward upon itself (*incurvatus in se ipsum*). And this curved self can only be made straight, and directed to an object appropriate to its realization of the self's destiny in God, if the love of God is a desire that reigns over all others. "Thou hast formed us for thyself, O Lord, and our hearts are restless till they rest in thee."

Now therefore, brothers and sisters, let us so love that object of the heart's affections which is able ultimately to straighten out our bendable wills that we may so make our way with fear and trembling amidst all the seductive sausages of this world

75

that we come not to futility and destruction. For the only love that can satisfy the fire of love with which God has endowed his children is not any of the various loves we love, but the ineffable love with which we are eternally beloved.

The Mad Obedience
God Requires

The Sermon on the Mount seems to present a desirable—and impossible—situation. The Speaker intended an explosive result—and nineteen hundred years have confirmed his success. As we ponder both the capacity of humans to hear God speak and the demonic human capacity to settle for less than the mad obedience God requires, the form of utterance in these commands will appear as the only conceivable way the Word of God to such as we are could be conveyed. In support of that assertion the following propositions are submitted:

1. An absolute demand is the only verbal form by which to announce and release an indeterminate power, communicate an indeterminate promise, diagnose and judge our indeterminate ability to deceive and excuse ourselves, enunciate an indeterminate possibility.

2. To be called to stand under the will of God as absolute demand is the only possibility by which to hold lives unconditionally responsible to God, the only way fully to celebrate the godliness of God.

3. To have to live under the absolute demand is the only way, given the human power of dissimulation and self-deception, to keep life taut with need, open to God's power, under judgment by his justice, indeterminately dependent upon his love, forgiveness, and grace.

4. To have to stand under God's absolute demand is the only way to keep us open to forms and occasions of obedience that the emerging and unpredictable facts of our involvement in social change constantly present to us for obedience. Even relative obedience, that is to say, can only sustain itself in the light of the absolute demand.

5. Only the absolute demand can sensitize human beings to

occasions for ethical work and energize them toward even relative achievements. And only such a demand can deliver us, in these achievements, from complacency and pride, prevent us from making an identification of human justice with the justice of God.

6. Only the absolute demand has the transcendent freedom to stride forever out in front of all human accomplishments, fresh and powerful with the lure of deeper and more comprehensive goals.

7. The historical-relative requires the Godly-absolute even to see and to seek the better in the existing. Any understanding of the good without God will cease even to be good. Cut off from the absolute, the relative ossifies into pride, becomes inert in the memory of past achievements, or makes a sardonic idol out of more and more smooth and profitable adjustments in the social order.

Van Gogh and an Old Pair
of Shoes

In the words of Richard Wilbur, human beings have always tended to "guard and gild what's common." To inquire with the mind why they do that, and rejoice with delight and a lifting of the heart because they do it, is to place oneself at the center of a "sense for the world." We want to ask, for instance, what it means that Van Gogh so paints a pair of old shoes that there is evoked from the beholder a deep sense of both the terror and the dignity of our common humanity, and a smiling sense of our fellowship with it; that Edward Hopper can so paint a figure enclosed in solitariness, sitting upon a stool in a garish, neon-brilliant corner of an all-night eating joint starkly contrasted with the immense darkness of the midnight city, that the call of loneliness to loneliness is "guarded and gilded" in an iconography of recognition; that in all ages mighty works of literature, says Arthur Quiller-Couch, "traffic not with cold, celestial certainty, but with men's hopes and fears and breakings of the heart, all that gladdens, saddens, maddens us men and women in this brief and mutable traject" of life in the creation which is our home for a while, the anchorage of our actual selves.

Nature and grace, perception, experience, and wonder, the creation as the habitat of our bodies, and the divine redemption as the Word of God to our spirits, must all be held together in thought as indeed they occur together in fact. And if, in the elaboration of this notion, the sober statement of the artist is adduced as useful, the absence of a theological label upon such evidence is of no significance. If the occasions of grace, both in Israel's experience and in the testimony of the Christian community, are incarnate—for Israel in its historical experience of liberation and God-heldness, for the Christian community in the "glory" of God beheld in "the face of Christ Jesus"—the place of grace must be the webbed connectedness of our creaturely life. That web does not indeed bestow grace; it is necessarily the theater for that anguish and delight, that maturation of longing and hope, that solidification of knowledge that can attain, as regards ultimate issues, not a clean, crisp certainty but rather the knowledge that, in the words of W. H. Auden,

> We who must die demand a miracle.
> How could the Eternal do a temporal act,
> The Infinite become a finite fact?
> Nothing can save us that is possible:
> We who must die demand a miracle.*

This turning to experience is not a way to account for grace; it may well be a prolegomenon to the possibility of what Karl Rahner calls a "transcendental anthropology," by a way artists affirm in their own concrete and earthy visions. Joseph Conrad, for instance, in his preface to *The Nigger of the Narcissus:*

> He [the artist] speaks to our capacity for delight and wonder, to the sense of mystery surrounding our lives; to our sense of pity, and beauty, and pain; to the latent feeling of fellowship with all creation—and to the subtle but invincible conviction of solidarity that knits together the loneliness of innumerable hearts, to the solidarity in dreams, in joy, in sorrow, in aspirations, in illusions, in hope, in fear, which binds men to each other, which binds together all humanity—the dead to the living and the living to the unborn.

Or Henry James in *The Art of Fiction:*

> Experience is never limited and it is never complete, it is an immense sensibility, a kind of huge spiderweb of the finest silken threads suspended in the chamber of consciousness, and catching every airborne particle in its tissue.

The World of a 747 Pilot

Many a person of our time might be designated as Homo operator—one whose procedures are often at a distance, removed from actual things, people, purposes. Such a person sits at a desk covered with papers that represent things, not at a bench covered with real things. Actualities appear in their mathematized or otherwise symbolized equivalents. This teller, broker, retailer, distributor, operator of a part of a system may sit in an office in Boston and sell state of Maine potatoes, which he or she has never seen, to a wholesaler who is an ''account'' and a voice on the telephone and who lives in Chicago.

The pilot of a modern aircraft is Homo operator in an almost absolute sense. Every natural reality that makes the plane go and holds it aloft arrives to the pilot's sense and procedure via gauges, indicators, lights, and meters. Numbers tell the state of the airy world: elevation, velocity, the condition or status of engine, wing, tail, fuel, and water. Distance is transposed into time: Atlanta is ninety minutes from Chicago. Visual fact is transposed into interpretive signals on a dial; the actual and the responses necessary to conform to it are taken out of the agency of personal judgment and transferred to computerized adjustments appropriate to a complex of factors that require neither hands nor eyes.

The point here has nothing to do with the value, trustworthiness, or even the necessity of such instrumentation of natural fact. The point is rather to enforce the truth of the argument that technology as such, and quite apart from one's assessment of its promises and perils, profoundly changes Homo operator's sense for the world. One is reminded of Paul Tillich's ''technical reason,'' which provides means for ends but provides no guidance for the evaluation of ends. Production, or plain continued operations, become frantically involved with ever more sophisticated means, and the tools which are used in the process create a "second nature" above physical nature which subjects humans to itself and proves as unpredictable and destructive as nature itself. Indeed, there have been perceptive questions as to why the recent vehement determination of the young to change the priorities of America's national life has so precipitously collapsed. The force of Tillich's assertion that technology injects a "second nature" into humanity's reflective life is certified by a typical student outburst: "What can we do? Where can we grab hold of what's fixed and set and rolling along? The whole damned thing has a life of its own; it runs by itself!"

This changed sense for the world demands two quite fresh responses to a universe so organized in mind and practice. The first of these is a vast expansion of the notion of nature. For the reference of the term must now go beyond the given nonhuman world of land and sea and forest and wind and rain and petroleum and the entire range of plant and animal life. Homo operator is as ultimately dependent upon this primal nature as humanity has always been; but the *sense* for this dependence is distanced and muted in virtue of the astounding transformations science-based technology has wrought. The "made" world that has come into being following the work of the chemist, the physicist, the biologist, the engineer is closer to the common life of the millions than the "natural" world of our fathers. Forests meet us as paper and plywood; oil and coal as energy, Saran wrap, tires, and pharmaceuticals.

Nor can the argument that this transformed, artifactual world constitutes a primary factor in contemporary estrangement really be sustained. There is estrangement, to be sure, but observation forces one to locate its causes elsewhere. For so adaptable is humankind to the world science has made possible and technology has realized that in this new, "made," extrapolated world most persons feel at home. Here they "belong" in the company of fellow operators in the world, they find a "natural" community; here they feel secure, for they know the rules of the game; here they see and work with astounding fabrications out of primal nature and confront these fabrications with familiar, even playful recognition.

If, then, we are required to expand our notion of the natural to include human transformation of it, we are also required to relate grace to nature in ways appropriate and adequate to nature so understood and so brought within humanity's operational existence. The advancement of this theological task cannot be accomplished by theology working in a specialized, reconceptualizing disengagement from other areas of human sensibility.

For the reality of grace must be encountered, specified, named, and known in whatever perceptions carry upon and within themselves the impact and quality that resonates back to that fountain, origin, and actor-in-grace who, in the tradition, is called "the God of Abraham, Isaac and Jacob" and "the Father of our Lord Jesus Christ." This interior resonance of recognition, begetting or evoking praise and thanksgiving, is a function of the particularity of grace itself. For grace has its marks. Whenever humans encounter grace, it is the shock and the overplus of sheer gratuity that announces the presence, as indeed it invented the name. By gratuity is meant a primal surprise, the need-not-have-been of uncalculated and incalculable givenness. "Amazing" is the only adequate adjective; wonder is the ambience. For amazement, wonder, and grace occur together. "They were amazed at the graciousness of his words."

But the very capacity for wonder can become calloused, covered over with the scar tissue that forms when experience abounds in the new, the marvelous, the fantastic. The operational person presents a hard case for the voices in our day that plead for a "rebirth of wonder." A generation reared on the TV extravaganza has been so visually and aurally bombed and banalized that efforts to reach and touch into life the shrunken sense of gratuity must find fresh ways. There can be no doubt that the church, the community that lives by the recognition of grace, is beginning to understand this and grope for such ways as shall celebrate the "difference" in its sense for the world and signalize this known difference by exterior signs. The movement is all in one direction—to announce the amazing in, with, and under the common; to beckon to wonder via the close and the usual; to divest the wonderful of the habiliments of elegance and reclothe adoration in simplicity. In architecture the churches cannot out-big the world; therefore the direct, the honest, the unostentatious. In vestments the church cannot out-do Countess Mara; therefore the plain bluntness of common texture. In the language of worship the church cannot any longer allure by sonorities of the half-understood; therefore the crispness of clear statement. There is a student congregation known to me in which the general prayer is responded to no longer with the traditional "Amen" but by the rejoinder "We really mean it!" It is not likely that so ordinary a transposition could become liturgically established, but the clarity of the response, so obviously appropriate to the meaning of the word "Amen," is a finger pointing in the right direction.

This movement toward the domestication of the occasions of grace is neither a denial of its source in God nor a diminishment of its power; it is rather a relocation of the encounter amidst those operations which constitute the level usualness of lived reality. It is a fresh realization of the deeply evangelical truth that the Incarnation of grace, precise in a person, is creative of a sense for the world which is total in its scope, near at hand in its invitation to recognition, adoration, and service, and beseeches and judges us in infinite love through the mortal eyes of human need.

The critical problem of Jesus' use of the "Son of man" term cannot be used to evade the terrible clarity of Matthew 25:31ff.

For it is God the Father who here assesses and judges. When the Father's blessing is declared upon those who cared for the hungry, thirsty, lonely, naked, sick, imprisoned, and when, astonished, people asked where and when it was that the Father was thus encountered, the identification of a gracious God with human anguish is absolute. "I tell you this: anything you did for one of my brothers here, however humble, you did for me."

To relegate this saying to the field of ethics is a fateful misunderstanding. For the reality of grace is not severable from that web and bundle of life out of which the human emerges and is defined, within which the negatives of need and anguish and death as well as the affirmative vitalities of beauty and joy burst forth, to which the Incarnation of grace came, and which, in the numberless occasions of experience, constitutes the theater of our redemption by grace.

Lake Michigan and Grace

In the course of his journey to Jerusalem he was travelling through the borderlands of Samaria and Galilee. As he was entering a village he was met by ten men with leprosy. They stood some way off and called out to him, "Jesus, Master, take pity on us." When he saw them he said, "Go and show yourselves to the priests"; and while they were on their way they were made clean.

(Luke 17:11-14 NEB)

This New Testament episode makes the point that action may sensitize cognition. We do not do what we should only after we are clear about all the facts; we also learn about facts when we go the way we must. The doing of the required illuminates and multiplies the possible; it draws the mind forward into fresh cognitions. Walking where one "has to go" discloses hitherto unregarded relations. The incessant pressure of the question "What ought I to do?" decisively modifies and opens the epistemological question "What can I know?" The ten lepers were cleansed "on the way" to an indeterminate and clinically absurd obedience. As old as Augustine is the relation between how I regard a thing and what is possible to know about a thing. Love opens to knowledge. *Non intradit veritatem nisi per caritatem*—there is no entrance to truth save by love.

This symbiotic coexistence and interaction of the risk of faith, the consequent investiture of the creation with a gracious possibility in virtue of the Incarnation of grace in time, space, matter ("born of woman, crucified under Pontius Pilate"), and an ethicizing of our regard for and our transactions with nature as *still*, despite human rapacity and despoliation, a field of grace—this is proposed as a Christian theological pattern of a magnitude that matches the misery of our environmental debacle.

Can the affirmation that God is gracious, and that God's

creation must be enjoyed and used as a gracious gift, have the power to accomplish that radical change in "the spirit of our minds" that the problem of humanity and environment demands? Two considerations are in order as we ask that question.

First, if the Christian community is to go beyond a mere adding of its numerically modest voice to the urging of that issue, that community under the guise of public morality will betray its responsibility. A change in the "spirit of our minds" requires something vastly more than a combination of frightening facts and moral concern. There is sufficient evidence that human beings are quite capable of marching steadily into disaster fully equipped with the facts. Pride, comfort, and an idolatrous and brutal hardness of heart have for several generations permitted the American nation to stare straight into the face of poverty, injustice, and the calcified privilege of the powerful—and leave national priorities unchallenged.

Against that realization one must assess accurately the sanguine assumption that knowledge of fact can by itself create change. Fundamental changes are evaded by the dramatization of small ones; faults at the center of a system are obscured or dismissed by cosmetic operations on the surface. A political and an economic system develops a rhetoric of celebration about its accomplishments that is capable of an act of seduction on a national scale. Rigor mortis is celebrated as stability.

Ecological rationality and the creation of public law appropriate to justice and care for the clear and clamant needs of persons—these right ends of social purpose are regularly shattered against inherited and clearly no longer effective laws governing uses of property, the exercise of legally defended autonomy in land use, and definitions of corporate responsibility bent to the advantage of the strong.

The second consideration is this: the Christian community exists in the power of events, presences, and visions that are betrayed when its total and holy understanding of the person and God, the person and the neighbor, the person and God's creation are translated down from their fiercely elevated and dynamic, steadily revolutionary reality. That the care of the earth is rational, necessary, aesthetic—the convulsive and renovating and never-to-be-quieted torment and glory of the story of God and Abraham, God and Jesus Christ, God and our recalcitrant spirits does not have to be invoked for that. The community of the people of God, who live by and are held within God's grace, has another and wilder thing to do. This is a people caught and held by a vision of a King, a kingdom, and a consummation—and by the massive contexts of culture, history, nature as fields of its holy disturbance.

It is not an accidental fact that utopias have been formulated only where the historical dynamism inseparable from Christian faith has been exercised. But there is a decisive difference between utopias and the visions of human life and possibility that the faith relentlessly explodes into fresh forms. Utopias owe their character and force to the vigor of the "see what is possible!"

The Christian vision is fundamentally different; its vision of what is possible is engendered both by the realities of human existence and the promises of the God of its faith. Christian vision believes out of both possibility and promise. Its fundamental trust is not in the allure or energy of the possible (these collapse, wane, frustrate) but in the Giver and Promiser who does not abandon what he has given or renounce his promises. Just as one's hope for eternal life in God is a correlate of the reality of the promises of the God of faith—and does not ultimately rest upon either human desire or human hope—so our vision of the new creation is a product of God who is affirmed in faith to be a Creator of the world, Redeemer of the world, and Sanctifier of the world.

The one comprehensive reality of this Trinitarian God is grace; the place of encounter with this grace of the Triune God is the given and modified arena of creation, the alienated arena of redemption, the envisioned arena of the future of humanity, the Spirit, and the world.

Is there, however, apart from the sheer momentum inherent in the reality of grace itself and the formal necessity to postulate the grace of the one God as present and at work in the work and presence of the one God, evidence from the facts of life that faith's investiture of everything experienced and reflected about with the supreme meaning-as-grace is an intelligible act?

I am talking now about ethicality and verification. By ethicality is meant the necessity for the organization of life toward continuation, care, and enhancement if life is to be at all. That life is like that and that its fundamental drive is in that direction I take to be nonarguable datum. There is an issue which, regardless of what scientist or philosopher may think, cannot be left hanging for faith. When grace is postulated as the reality of God, as the reality of the life of the Father in the Son witnessed to by the "internal testimony of the Holy Spirit," then literally all that is must be invested with an interpretation congruent with that postulate. By ethicality, then, is meant not only a way of acting in accord with and as an actualization of that faith, but a way of understanding that begets the possibility to assess all things from that center.

By verification is meant a warrant for the adequacy, coherence, and truth of such an understanding. What warrant is there for such a faith-investiture? What evidence from the world of fact invites the mind to suppose and supports the mind in supposing that the grace of the Creator is a principle of the creation; that a primal regard for things in terms of the marvel and particularity of their "being there" at all is somewhat more than an imposition, or an unwarranted extrapolation from the superheated theological fancy untroubled by intrusions of verifiable fact?

89

If things cannot continue to be at all except people relate to them with due regard for their given structure and need, then there is certainly rational warrant that assessment of things according to their transutilitarian "good" is an appropriate recognition of an intrinsic "good" in things that are. If a postulate about the source, status, and transpersonal actuality of the world-as-nature (that it is of God, and a theater of his grace) begets an assessment of that world and a consequent use of it consistent with the assessment, then by an empiricism-of-outcomes, the postulate is logically and experientially warranted. Or, to put the proposal another way: what is necessary for the continued existence of things and essential to prevent the perversion or distortion of the given nature of things may be reasonably postulated as congruent with the truth of things. Indeed, this "postulate" moves toward the status of a principle if conditions for the very existence of persons and things are *absolute* conditions.

If the realm of nature is regarded and used under the rubric of grace, and responds as if one had discovered its true name, and along with God's human creation "delights" to have a name and to have been given freedom to be, the ancient image of "the morning stars sang together, and all the sons of God shouted for you" returns with something more than poetic force. If, for instance, Lake Michigan is assessed according to its given ecological structure as a place for multiple forms of life, by nature self-sustaining and clean, available for right use and delight, then in a blunt and verifiable way we are "justified" by grace even in our relation to the things of nature. The opposite of justification is condemnation, and there is an empirically verifiable condemnation that works out its slow but implacable judgment in the absence of such "gracious" regard for nature. If a lake becomes a disposal resource, or a dump, or a means for cooling ingots, or a bath to flush out oil bunkers (both instances proper to legitimate use and technically subject to restoration to

90

cleanliness), then a repudiated grace that "justifies" becomes the silent agent of condemnation.

> For he has made known to us in all wisdom and insight the mystery of his will, according to his purpose which he set forth in Christ, as a plan for the fullness of time, to unite all things in him, things in heaven and things on earth.
>
> (Eph. 1:9–10)

The Bill Is Due and Payable

Can a mentality and spirit nurtured upon the availability of open space even envision, much less attack, the tasks that now confront us? Can the indubitable spiritual energies called forth and shaped by a frontier circumstance be informed, disciplined, reformed, and released for a future whose setting is a radically different one? Operations in new space make appropriate and effective a manner of public order that is pragmatic; can operations in a closely woven, ecologically integrated, and delicate structure be rightly guided by the same cast of mind? Is the institutionalization of materialism an adequate public philosophy for circumstances which in a thousand large and small particulars are new? Can the spirit that won a continent sustain a national society?

The answer, in my judgment, is clearly no. But the structure of spirit which in the new situation must, in St. Paul's phrase, constitute the "spirit of our minds" must now be explicated as over against that structure of spirit which has until now been most determinative of our nation.

Human beings live in space and time. These dimensions of actual existence are profound spiritual symbols, and reflection upon them as they penetrate and fructify the critical intelligence bestows both cognitive sensibility and power. Just as life-in-space is at one phase of a people's life educative for the achievement of right order, so too the reality of life-in-time is in a later phase educative to right order. The maturation of societies in space may, at a certain phase of unfolding, be so dramatic a fact that the society can ignore, set aside, or in the exuberance of its expansion repudiate the lurking and ultimately unavoidable requirements placed upon humanity by that other dimension of historical reality, life-in-time. Space offers options that may be realized by moving; time stands as a symbol for that historical accomplishment of order which is achieved by decisions made where one is. Space may operate to confront issues by flight; time is the symbol of that boundedness within which the less dramatic, tougher, but ultimately more human society is attempted by the discipline of the spirit, the perception of human values, and decisions proper to such values. The new time-consciousness makes demands of us that are in clear opposition to the popularly celebrated momentum of our history—a less aggressive notion of maturity, a tenderer and more complex notion of order, a more intellectual concept of discipline, an ecologically embedded idea of choice.

The spirit of the person who looks out upon the future in space and the spirit of the person who looks inward upon the issues of right order for human life in space and time—this difference is too eloquent for abstraction. Contrast with Walt Whitman's space-singing verse another American song of a generation later, George Santayana's "Cape Cod":

The low sandy beach and the thin scrub pine,
The wide reach of a bay and the long sky line,—
  O, I am far from home.

The salt, salt smell of the thick sea-air,
And the smooth round stones that the ebb-tides wear,—
  When will the good ship come?

The wretched stumps all charred and burned,
And the deep soft rut where the cartwheel turned,—
  Why is the world so old?

The lapping wave and the broad gray sky,
Where the cawing crows and the slow gulls fly,—
  Where are the dead untold?

The thin slant willows by the flooded bog,
The huge stranded hulk and the floating log,—
  Sorrow with life began!

And among the dark pines, and along the flat shore,
O the wind, and the wind, forevermore,—
What will become of man?

The American epic has come, such a contrast would power-
fully suggest, to a crisis in the very spirit of our minds. We have,
while solving some problems, ignored others. We have fash-
ioned a society and an industrial order at a cost, and the bill is
due and payable. The magnificence of our endowment has been
cleverly used and appallingly abused. The accumulated garbage
of the achievement has befouled the air, polluted the water,
scarred the land, besmirched the beautiful, clogged and con-
fused our living space, so managed all human placement and
means of movement as to convenience us as consumers and in-
sult us as persons.

The character of a people's life-experience in a particular
place profoundly influences their permeability to the
eschatological reality, proclaimed by biblical faith and catholic
tradition, that life in historical time has problems that cannot be
confronted and promises that cannot be fulfilled by sheer movement in space. And precisely that is the innermost content of
this moment's mood in our national life. We are puzzled,
bewildered, and annoyed by new requirements for which old
reactions are useless. The problems of the city are not soluble by
flight; the problem of poverty is apparently not soluble in
human terms within the pattern of an economic system whose
very successes have become deepeningly unjust; the problem of
education is not soluble by present provisions that do not
recognize the damage done to human beings by past deprivation. What is tragic and frightening about this moment is that
its enormous possibility for a better, more humane, richer,
fuller-dimensional future for American life is most often interpreted in negative terms. A riot fired by intolerable conditions
that persist by sheer stasis when wealth is available to correct

them is interpreted simply as a breakdown of law and order! It is
that; but the human breakdown is deeper and holier; it is a cry
whose substance is older than law and whose passion is for order
congruent with human need.

A Soggy Piety

Dealing with problems that arise out of piety is like throwing a baseball at a feather pillow; it just sinks in and disappears, absorbed by sogginess. And soggy piety is, unhappily, one form of piety. I meet it, for example, in people who, following a talk about the Christian responsibility for the care of the earth, will remark: "I hear what you say, it is very serious and we must do something about it; but I really trust in the Lord. The Lord will not permit us to do this to his world. This is our Father's world and he will see to it that we do not destroy it." The first person who said this to me took me rather aback because I had not met that one before. But neither, of course, had I met before the kind of a jovial God who lets you romp all over his garden and will clean up the garbage after you have messed it up. I was hard put for a moment—but by providential help, for only a moment.

I remembered a wonderful passage in the prophets—you remember—where God is talking to a prophet who has worked very hard at a certain vocation and has become quite discouraged. The prophet is taking the matter up with God and says, "I seem to be working hard at it, but I'm not getting anywhere." And God says, "I will send my servant Nebuchadnezzar." And the prophet says, "How's that again? That guy? You really mean you are going to let Nebuchadnezzar serve your purposes?" God says, "You heard me! I will send *my* servant Nebuchadnezzar."

So not all the purposes of God are realized in the hands of the church, but God is a God of judgment as well as of grace; you cannot get away endlessly with rapacity toward his creation.

I Still Plant Trees

If the object of Christian hope is God, this means that Christian hope is not a devout function of an evaluation of history. That is, some people evaluate history as moving, maybe in a jerky and oscillating fashion, toward a broader humanity, a deeper justice, a more caring relation with the environment, a greater intimacy between persons. That depends, I suppose, on how you read it. I do not hope in these things in the sense that I "hope in God." If anything is going to be redemptive, it will have to be in virtue of God in strange ways working out his purposes with his creation which, it is my faith, he does not abandon. So my hope is in God; I have literally no hope, in the same qualitative sense, in historical procedures. This does not mean I do not have certain observations which I think indicate that we are moving well here or badly there; and I greet all advances, as I see them, with joy, and I lament the recessions. But in a general sense, the big word "hope" I would not apply to historical observations.

I do not think we are in a very good situation historically. For instance, I do not believe that our relationship to the earth is liable to change for the better until it gets catastrophically worse. Our record indicates that we can walk with our eyes wide open straight into sheer destruction if there is a profit on the way—and that seems to me to be what we are doing now. I have no great expectation that human cussedness will somehow be quickly modified and turned into generosity or that humanity's care of the earth will improve much.

But I do go around planting trees on the campus.

The Erosion of Communities

Hannah Arendt, in her book of some years ago called *The Human Condition*, says that the problem of finding satisfactory communities is exacerbated in the twentieth century because we have witnessed the erosion, if not the annihilation, of the natural forms of community. These natural forms, which for hundreds of years remained strong and withstood all kinds of change, were the community of national identity, the community of the family, the community of work, and the community of a remembered past. All these natural forms of community have undergone awesome shocks. The national community is now eclipsed by internationalism, which is probably good. The sense of family indentity, as we all know, has become obscured. The community of work, in which people once met all day long in a common task as artisans, purveyors, or whatever, has radically changed. Nor do we any longer come together to shuck corn, raise houses, put up tomatoes, or prepare the turkey dinner.

The frenzy with which we seek to replace these communities is a tribute to their importance and a recognition of the loss we have suffered by their erosion. The message is clear: without community there is no person. What God has joined together, let no human being put asunder. Personhood is a social state, so we desperately grope for communities. And these sought-after communities are expected to supply highly charged moments instead of experiences quietly spread over a long period of time. A church conference or retreat is a good example. When persons come together on Friday night and leave again on Sunday afternoon, they must compress the whole process of knowledge, intimacy, and self-disclosure; this compression can lead easily to manipulation.

The Christian community ought to be more than that, and its

particularity will be exposed when the commitment to the church's story creates a coming-together that is ostensibly, visibly different. Its operation is different too. The church cannot affirm itself into particularity; it will have to act so that the difference is obvious. I think it is Gibbon who said, "The early church outlived, outthought, and outdied the pagan world. They lived better, they were more moral, just, and honest." That is what called the attention of the pagan world to the little Christian community.

The church in the next several decades is going to be a smaller, leaner, tougher company. I am convinced that the way for the church now is to accept the shrinkage, to penetrate the meaning and the threat of the prevailing secularity, and to tighten its mind around the task given to the critical cadre.

Community as a Problem

It is simply not true, as is widely affirmed these days, that the matrix of close human relationships is a theater within which fulfillment is guaranteed. Close relationships do provide an important resource—one of which we could probably use more. But there is a time when it simply will not do to declare such human bonds as the absolute, ultimate resource of the Christian gospel. There is, finally, a loneliness in every human life; I am simply not impressed with the promise that happiness in human existence will devolve from the mutuality of personal relationships. Such connections are not fulfilling; in fact, if I could push my thesis further, I would say that the community can actually get in the way by *promising* fulfillment. Fulfillment is finally not possible in human existence. That is why we have a gospel of divine redemption.

Because human relationships have a limit, and because even the most powerful of them leaves individual solitude uninvaded, the gospel of the divine redemption carries so astounding a promise. Is it not possible that this promise constitutes the allure of the phrase from the confessional prayer " . . . and from whom no secrets are hid"?

A Proper Love of One's Country

Before the word *America* can set one thinking or planning or resolving or defending, it ought to set one dreaming and remembering. And out of this dreamed procession of America as a concrete place will be poured the ingot of a tough and true patriotism. Have you who read these lines never gone inwardly wandering among the myriad impacts of this magnificent land?—the sprawling, opulent South of the stark red earth and the blithe and lazy skies; the tragic, lonely beauty of New England, its neat white houses and stone fences, so proper to its prim certainty; the sweep of the Middle West with its little towns set astride ten thousand Main Streets that become white concrete ribbons stretching across a countryside of incredible fertility and scope; the terrifying distances of the western states where farmers' families of a Saturday night still "run into town"—eighty miles—with insouciant ease; and the fabulous West Coast, majestic at the top where Rainier sparkles, rich and worldly-wise at the center where the land enfolds in long arms the lovely bay, and the fantastic glitter and brashness at the bottom where sprawls and brawls the City of the Angels.

Our American lives are impoverished if they lack a sense of identity with the country around them and are ignorant of its written and anecdotal history. The rootlessness of American life finds in such ignorance a part of its cause. We sit lightly to places and people; we are in large part a migrant population. Frontier psychology has persisted beyond the disappearance of the frontier. We *belong* to many things; few of us retain a sense of belonging to a particular place or a pattern of life. No wonder then that a corporation chartered in Delaware, doing business in Ohio, directed from New York can airily transfer members of its staff from New Jersey to Illinois without batting an eye over the human dislocations involved.

Loving, personal identification with one's own land has never been a breeder of arrogant nationalism. Indeed, a person's love for his or her own land can be the basis of respect for other people's love of their land. Just as only those who have convictions know the meaning of tolerance, so none can assess at right value the land-loves of other people except those who know and deeply love their own.

God

For many persons the word *God* is forever trapped within negative—often adolescent—understanding. Adult suspicion of religious reality is often rooted ín early and unpleasant experiences. I have met so many people who in growing up heard the word God as an almost pure, holy name for coercion, negation, and limitation. If an individual has found in the experience of growing up that the word God meant a no to every creative possibility, a club held over the head of anything that was any fun, then the first job for us to undertake is a dry cleaning of the term itself. It would be necessary to ask the individual what he or she might understand by the concept of faith. In letting the person talk, it might be apparent that faith is understood as *(a)* an optimism that will not bear very much examination, or *(b)* a sentimentalism that cracks to pieces on the rocks of life, or *(c)* an intellectual stupor that can only be maintained because the person never asks any serious questions. Now all of these have got to be disclosed in their own inadequacy—indeed their falsity—before the possibility is open for a truer, profounder, and more inclusive notion of what the word God has meant for hundreds of years to thousands of people.

If we're going to operate with the word God at all, then we had better be pretty clear about it. Not in the sense that we can define it and nail it down. But we can point in the direction of that which is before or more than or underneath—creating all of life. Some years ago there was a book published entitled *The Death of God.* And it found an immediate popularity because it hit an exposed nerve: the word God had been divested of any clear meaning, and at long last somebody had said it out loud and millions said, ''Amen, God is dead.'' What they meant was that the inherited notion of God which in the religious fifties was widespread, with God as a kind of guarantor of our satisfaction with the status quo, an eternal protector of our particular life-style and our way of doing business, is dead. The death of that kind of god is a great gain, because the phony must die in order that the real can emerge. But when people say "God is dead" and really mean it, they ought to quit thinking about it and talking about it. The odd thing is, though, that God, who is loudly acclaimed to be dead, has a strange career in that the idea of his death is both incredible and undismissible. Now to think that it is both incredible and undismissible, regardless of what else you might think, is important. If I can neither clarify a thing nor get rid of it, then it is disturbing at a very deep level.

Moses was a man who had a task placed on him; he didn't say it was by God, but he had a task which was to liberate his people from a political and economic tyranny. By being faithful to what he was called on to do, he led them out of their oppression and captivity. Afterward he came to terms with what it was that made him do this, that made him feel like a traitorous heel if he didn't do it. He wandered around in the wilderness and he saw a bush that, in the terms of the old story, was ablaze but was not consumed. Moses talked about the experience as a symbol of both the incredibility and the undismissibility of the deepest motivations in life. And he called his awareness "God."

Now when we use the word God, as when that old story uses the word God, we are referring to that which constitutes the very life of life itself, that which is the mystery just beyond the boundary of everything we can figure out. It is the fundamental motivation that keeps pushing us in directions we don't want to go, asking questions which logically we ought to dismiss, probing at problems of which other people will say, "If you can't answer it, quit fooling around with it." But if we are bothered by something that profound, then we are well advised not to dismiss it.

I don't know that God "exists." That's why I begin Sunday morning like so many other people by saying, "I believe in God the Father Almighty, Maker of heaven and earth." I don't know that he exists in any way that would make sense in other uses of the words *I know*. I *know* that I came over here in a car this morning. I *know* that I had an appointment at eight o'clock, and I *know* that I had a coffee with you ten minutes ago. I trust the reliability of my memory on good empirical grounds. It has served me trustworthily in the past: I have no reason to think it is fooling me about what I did this morning. But if you say, "How do you *know* that God exists?" I cannot use the word *know* in the ways I just used it. I believe that he exists, but is this a sheer act of will, of "the will to believe," as Will James puts it? No, it is not.

Let me phrase it this way: Christian faith is an act of our total selves whereby on the ground of revelation, tradition, and our own experience we make "a leap of faith," as Kierkegaard called it. By this leap we find reality and meaning in what otherwise would remain unknown. And we use the largest symbol possible for this reality and call it God. The truth of this cannot be proven, and yet, on the other hand, there is a way of making powerful claims for the Christian faith.

If I deal with myself, my neighbor, and the world as if God does exist, the outcome of that dealing will be in the direction of the preservation and enhancement of self, neighbor, and world. If I do not do that, we're all on the way to destruction. Such a mode of thought and action is an empiricism of outcomes. It's looking at what would be the result of another position. For instance, I know that a particular piece of land or forest will continue to be a viable woodland and a habitat for animals if I treat it in a certain way. But if I treat it in another way, it will cease to be a viable forest. Then I have a rational right to say there's something in the nature of things that demands care and love.

Now that's a funny kind of proof. On the other hand, it's a very powerful kind of proof because it's a proof that's based on what maintains, what sustains, what enhances, what tends toward the fulfillment of things. And if love does that, then love is not just an affection. It may indeed be true as Dante says when, reaching in the *Paradiso* for the foundational life of things, he talks of the love that holds the sun and all the other stars in heaven. Love may be the fundamental principle of the creation as well as that which makes human life possible.

Joy

Joy and happiness are different. Happiness depends very much on the fortunes of circumstance. Things turn out well or badly. One is happy in marriage, or happy in a job, or unhappy with a group of friends.

Joy persists almost independently of the waxings and wanings of circumstance. It is said of Jesus, "who for the joy that was set before him endured the cross"—a terrifying statement. I don't think we have any particular right to happiness, nor should we make it the goal of life. Joy is another thing; joy is never an achievement. It is that quality which comes to life only when one knows that the feverishness of happiness is not ultimately determined.

There is a kind of quiet, serene confidence in knowing that all things do not stand or fall according to one's own achievements or the correctness of every decision one makes. One has a kinship with a power beyond the self which is generative toward the good; one knows oneself to be placed within the sphere of that power and to be a part of it. There is also a kind of joy which may often have the face of tragedy. In fact, the very quality that permits a person to be open to joy also makes that person terribly vulnerable to the tragic. I know of no great spirit that has not been at the same time a tragic spirit. One recalls Goethe's words: "Who has not sat weeping through lonely nights has never sensed the heavenly mights."

The word *happiness* can be very deceptive—and the quest for it a perilous undertaking. The more you seek it, the less likely you are to find it, because the frenzy of the seeking cuts you off from that which might provide joy.

Guilt

Maybe a useful way to get at the nature of guilt would be by an analogy with fear. There are times when we are afraid and we know what we are afraid of. When the object of which we are afraid is clear, then it is possible to assess our situation and see whether our fear is justified or unjustified. But the kind of fear that really lays waste life is a generalized fear, an apprehension for which we cannot find an adequate object. It's as when a child wakes up at night crying and says, "I'm afraid." Mother comes in and asks, "What are you frightened about?" "I don't know, I'm just afraid." Now the only thing that will serve in a case like that is for the mother to say, "Don't be afraid, I'm here."

I think guilt has the same character. There is a special kind of guilt as when we neglect a specified duty or obligation, but there's also a generalized sense of guilt that pervades the whole of life and thought and being. And because we cannot specify what particular thing we are guilty about, the guilt remains unallayed. Now why do we have this generalized guilt? An answer is difficult to get at because the guilt itself is vaporous, elusive, yet nevertheless present in all experience. But where does it come from? It seems to me that a sense of guilt is built into the nature of the human being: the gap between the magnitude of possibility and the nature of achievement is always a big one.

The vision of what might have been and the record of what actually was are never identical. Those things that could have been done, ought to have been done, tasks and persons left unattended to—these make up a great part of our lives. Simply to cop out by finding good and sufficient reasons for not doing something in no way removes the generalized apprehension and guilt. I cannot think of any person, no matter how magnificent his or her achievement, who has not had the sense of coming short of what might have been. Renoir died thinking of the pictures he didn't paint, Michelangelo thought of the figures he didn't carve, Beethoven of the quartets he didn't write.

The Christian faith, and Judaism back of it, puts this feeling into a great phrase when it says, "We have all come short of the glory of God." The word "glory" there is a term that points to the largest, richest possible fulfillment of existence, existence which is talked about in terms of God because the glory of God is absolute identity between what might have been and what is. And we all come short of that. This kind of analysis of guilt indicates that guilt cannot be expunged from within its own dynamics.

Guilt cannot be resolved, but the fact is that something outside oneself must accept that which is unacceptable within oneself. The psychological magnitude of the Judeo-Christian faith is that it postulates a God who knows all about us, who knows specifically the reality of what to us remains always generalized. Therefore, only God's forgiveness is adequate to handle our guilt. It is not without significance that the old religious notion of forgiveness is that it goes beyond expiation; this is a forgiveness that deals with "those things which we ought not to have done and those things which we ought to have done."

An old liturgical confession talks about "secret thoughts and desires which I cannot fully understand, but which are all known unto thee." That's a magnificent statement because it says that before God, we do not lay out on the table all the specifiable failures of our lives and ask God to clean them up or forgive them: we never could clearly lay out on the counter all the stuff that's back on the subliminal shelf. Therefore those things "which I cannot fully understand, but which are all known unto thee." So that when guilt is analyzed and its permeation of the whole human situation is clearly seen, the relevance of the divine forgiveness is not only appropriate, but it alone is appropriate.

Acceptance

I think the word *acceptance* in our common conversations cannot be transferred from our ordinary speech about God. Because what we mean by acceptance in our human relationships is always an acceptance that depends upon mutuality. I can only be accepted if somehow I am found to be acceptable. In all our relationships, from the most intimate to the most casual, there are built-in tensions. I must to some degree *make* myself acceptable. We cannot move by an analogy from our acceptance of one another to what the New Testament means in saying that we are accepted by God. Our acceptance of God does not imply mutuality. It is a word spoken to us—and it is incredible. Our acceptance of each other, and even our acceptance of God, are always conditional acceptances. What marks the words *acceptance by God* is the unconditional fact that God accepts precisely the unacceptable. The holy accepts, goes after, and loves the sinner. The one who is the offended party initiates the action; so that when we talk of the divine acceptance, that's not the ambiguity and partiality of our human acceptance raised to the nth power. It is substantially different. That God accepts me is crazy. That I accept my neighbor is an act of humanly understandable generosity. But no understanding of this human meaning of acceptance ever adds up to, nor is it analogous to, divine acceptance.

You cannot move from the analysis of the ambiguity and the partiality of human acceptance to the divine acceptance; but you can move from the divine acceptance to a transformation of the possibilities of our human acceptances. The New Testament instructs us in "forgiving each other as the Lord has forgiven you." This means that the miracle of the divine acceptance, the amazing grace of it, can open us up and make us more generous, charitable, just, and accepting.

Validation

We can get a check validated, or a driver's license revalidated, but I think we have to ask the question, "Is life validatable within itself?" Another question is, "Are we seeking validation from around or validation from within?" Validation from around means that in order to be somebody or to feel comfortable with ourselves, we have to look horizontally around us and find some accepting relationships which validate us. In these acceptances there is some fulfillment, but I think we must ask the question of whether or not we can finally ever be validated by others. All such validations are both good and ultimately inadequate. We cannot find fulfillment from fellow persons only, regardless of the importance, the goodness, and the beauty of these relationships. We are really freed from the tyranny of having to be validated when we know that we cannot finally be validated by others.

The second kind of validation is sought within—that is, we try to find a self-image so secure and admirable that it needs no validation from around because it has adequate validation from the inside. This is the effort which emerges in the book *I'm OK—You're OK*. We seek to escape the horrendous notion that validation from within has perilous insufficiencies. George Santayana once said, "To be a fanatic is to redouble your efforts when you've forgotten your aim." Much of the frantic search for interior validation is a kind of whistling in the dark, but because of the ultimate negation, we always have to whistle louder. We have to anesthetize ourselves from the recognition that self-validation offers no lasting security. The keenness with which one peers within to secure self-validation will not stop when that pleasant result is achieved. The more penetrating the gaze, the less likely it is to come to a congratulatory stop at the boundaries of the self. For the one who gazes is a self among selves—a self in a great world pattern that transcends the self and, for any but the dullest spirit, will press toward the truth of total meaning. The momentum of the gaze that achieves the good of self-assessment leads toward a goal that transcends even a validated self.

The knowledge that validation by others or from within ourselves is inadequate can open us to a real form of validation. Judaism and Christianity point to one who is not one of our neighbors but who made all of our neighbors; he is the source of selves.

That which gave us life validates our life beyond the ability of our companions in life, or of our own introspection, to do the actual validation. There is in the Old Testament a word that says, "I have called you by your name, you are mine." This means that our name, which can be translated as our self-image and the community's opinion of us, is not fundamentally enough. Knowing *who* we are is a reality that depends finally on *whose* we are.

Christ and the Unity of His Church

When millions of the world's people, inside the church and outside of it, know that damnation now threatens nature as absolutely as it has always threatened humanity and societies in history, it is not likely that witness to a light that does not enfold and illumine the world-as-nature will be even comprehensible. For the root pathos of our time is the struggle by the peoples of the world in many and various ways to find some principle, order, or power which shall be strong enough to contain the raging "thrones, dominions, principalities" which restrict and ravage human life.

If to this longing of all persons everywhere we are to propose "him of whom, and through whom, and in whom are all things," then that proposal must be made in redemptive terms that are forged in the furnace of our crucial engagement with nature as both potential to blessedness and potential to hell.

The matter might be put another way: the address of Christian thought is weakest precisely where the human ache is most strong. We have had, and do have, a Christology of the moral soul, a Christology of history, and, if not a Christology of the ontic, affirmations so huge as to fill the space marked out by ontological questions. But we do not have, at least not in such effective force as to have engaged the thought of the common life, a daring, penetrating, life-affirming Christology of nature.

The theological magnificence of cosmic Christology lies, for the most part, still tightly folded in the church's innermost heart and memory. Its power is nascent among us all in our several styles of teaching, preaching, worship; its waiting potency is available for release in kerygmatic theology, in moral theology, in liturgical theology, in sacramental theology.

And the fact that our separate traditions incline us to one or another of these theologies as central does not diminish either the possibility of such a release, or our responsibility. For it is true of us all that the imperial vision of Christ as coherent in *ta panta* has not broken open the powers of grace to diagnose, judge, and heal the ways of humans as they blasphemously strut about this hurt and threatened world as if they owned it. Our vocabulary of praise has become personal, pastoral, too purely spiritual, static. We have not affirmed as inherent in Christ—God's proper person for humanity's proper selfhood and society—the world political, the world economic, the world aesthetic, and all other commanded orderings of actuality which flow from the ancient summons to tend this garden of the Lord. When atoms are disposable to the ultimate hurt then the very atoms must be reclaimed for God and his will.

The care of the earth, the realm of nature as a theater of grace, the ordering of bread and peace—these are christological obediences before they are practical necessities.

But if we are indeed called to unity, and if we can obey that call in terms of a contemporary Christology expanded to the dimensions of the New Testament vision, we shall perhaps obey into fuller unity. For in such obedience we have the promise of the divine blessing. This radioactive earth, so fecund and so fragile, is his creation, is our sister and the material place where we meet the brother in Christ's light. Ever since Hiroshima the very term *light* has had ghastly meanings. But ever since creation it has had meanings glorious; and ever since Bethlehem meanings concrete and beckoning.

Crucifixion

A cross is a blunt and graceless form. It has not the completeness and satisfying quality of a circle. It does not have the grace of a parabola or the promise of a long curve. A cross is a straight-up line abruptly crossed by a counterline. The assertive yes of its vertical is crossed and broken by the no of its horizontal. A cross speaks not of unity but of brokenness, not of harmony but of ambiguity; it is a form of tension and not of rest.

We humans know, surely, that there is an ultimate significance which is not identical with ourselves. But we are, nevertheless, quite unable to dethrone ourselves from the central position which we know we ought not to occupy. We try, indeed, in many ways; and our noblest effort goes by the name of religion. And it is precisely when the effort to remove ourselves from the center of all things has assumed the form of a high religion that we become most acutely conscious of the cruciform character of our moral situation. For in that effort we come to know, as Luther once put it, that "man seeks himself in everything, even in God."

It is precisely in the love relationship that the general enhancement of all reality has at its center a particular enhancement of myself, the lover. I love the beloved, but even more than that I love that vision of myself reflected back to me from the beloved at ten times its normal size. I love the beloved, but even more I love that discernment of my own lovableness on the part of the other by virtue of which that other responds to me!

And in the experience of prayer, too, one knows oneself to be in the presence of that "law in the members" of which Paul speaks. The life of prayer has been talked about with such unrealistic piety that one hesitates to point out that the unrealism of the speech often conceals the actual impiety which grounds even this good activity. For in prayer I have no sooner begun to address myself to God than I find myself commending myself for being in this attitude. I then condemn my commendation—and feel a positive virtue in having had sufficient perspicuity to see that I ought not to commend myself before God and in having condemned myself for so commending myself. But, I reason further, the very fact that I know I ought not to commend myself means that I myself in the depths of my being am not so bad a person after all. And so in moral oscillation between condemnation, which I commend, and commendation, which I condemn, I come to know that when St. Paul talked about the wretchedness of life's captivity he was not being simply autobiographical.

Because life itself is cruciform in character, it must be addressed, if it is to be savingly struck, in an action that itself is cruciform. Hence the majestic word of the Fourth Gospel, "The Word became flesh and dwelt among us." Flesh—because that is *what* we are. Dwelt among us—because that is *where* we are.

The task of theology is not to prove the Christian pronouncement by reference to categories outside itself; it is rather to describe God's Christ-deed in such a way that its relevance, judgment, and redemptive power become clear. When, therefore, in the areas of time, of moral reflection, and of self-realization we confront central pronouncements of the gospel, we arrive at the knowledge that something is here said which is startlingly relevant. It was a man who knew time in all of the fullness of its inner ambiguity who, caught up in the deed of Christ, was able to say, "We that love the Lord have passed from death to life . . . old things have passed away, all things are become new." And it was the same man who cried, not because he was ignorant of the Greek hope of immortality but in full consciousness of it, "Now unto the Blessed and only Potentate, King of Kings, Lord of Lords, who only hath immortality . . ."

And when humanity's moral consciousness has been viewed

in its ultimate nature and there revealed as Olympian, assertive, and always tyrannically egocentric, the word of the gospel is known to be the only word that God can speak to such a situation. I cannot be helped until I am related to God in a new way. I cannot perfect a structure on the existing foundation; new footings must be given. When Paul's cry, "O wretched man that I am, who shall deliver me from this body of death?" has passed from ancient autobiography to personal confession, then one is prepared to know that the word of forgiveness is the only word that is either redemptive or real. Hence the profound and everlasting rightness of the word of the gospel: "Son, thy sin be forgiven thee!"

•　　•　　•

The cross is the symbol because the whacks of life take that shape. Our lives are full of abandonments, infidelities, tragedies. The affirmation is always crossed by a negation. The vitalities of life move toward death. And unless you have a crucified God, you don't have a big enough God.

Death

The fear of death, I'm convinced, is at the bottom of all apprehensions. To say of any of us that we do not fear death is a lie. To be human is to fear death. To love life is to hope and to wish not to leave it. And all people fear death. I think that is one of the most creative fears there is because it bestows a value, an affection, and a gratitude for life which otherwise there would not be. That is what the Psalm (90) means by the statement "So teach us to number our days that we may get a heart of wisdom."

Why is it that in church we so seldom talk about this fear? I think it is because the churches have bought into the easy cultural attitude that we don't talk about unpleasant things. Our not talking about death leaves the subject up to others. Some poets have found a verbal way to pull the mask off this hidden subject. I think of Dylan Thomas's

> Do not go gentle into that good night.
> Rage, rage against the dying of the light.*

At the heart of the Christian message is the affirmation that God himself enters our dying—that God, the Creator of all things, the life of all life, has himself undergone that which is most common to us humans. The one of whom the church says, "In him is the fullness of God," not only died; he died a crucified convict. The Christian faith says that nothing in human experience is outside the experience of God. This means that the Christian faith does not abolish or eliminate the fear of death; rather it erects along with it the confession that God is

---

* Dylan Thomas, "Do Not Go Gentle Into That Good Night," *The Collected Poems of Dylan Thomas* (New York: New Directions, 1964), p. 128. Copyright 1946 by New Directions Publishing Corporation. Copyright 1952 by Dylan Thomas. Reprinted by permission of New Directions Publishing Corporation.

the life of life. God does not finally die. If any person's life be a participation in the eternal life of God, that person's life is also part of that which is not destroyed.

How this shall be is not made clear in the New Testament. When the Christian community asks Paul, "In what body shall the dead arise?" he adroitly avoids a concrete answer to a too-concrete question. Paul really does not give a blueprint of what the nature or circumstances of this life with God will be, but he wraps the thing up by saying, "If we live, we live to the Lord, and if we die, we die to the Lord; so then, whether we live or whether we die, we are the Lord's."

The point is that life, which comes from God, is cared for by God and somehow goes back into the life of God. And Paul seems to say: "For me that is enough. Whether I live or whether I die isn't really the great question. Let's move on to something important. How are you getting along over there?"

In a sense, aging is tutorial to the acceptance of one's own death because we do not die in a moment. Our personal world around us dies, so that we are instructed in the art of dying—the fathers used to call it *ars moriendi*. We are instructed in the fact and inevitability of our own death, and are invited to reflect upon our own death by the little deaths in our personal world. For example, I know that my life has been largely constituted by longtime relationships with dozens of persons who are not casual acquaintances but close working partners in theological and other tasks over the years. These, one by one, drop off. They are lost to me. These deaths are in a sense little personal deaths that I must undergo so that my own death becomes that toward which I naturally move and not just something I fear. In that sense I am not afraid of death, but I am afraid of dying.

The Christian faith is that if we live, we are the Lord's; if we die, we are the Lord's. This is a faith, not an empirically established truth. It is a statement about the meaningfulness of the Christian message which can only be established by faith.

The Christian church ought not only to refuse to buy so-called evidence for life after death; it should be the first to point out the very nervous kind of logic in such notions.

Empiricism involved with this idea is quite irrelevant to what the Christian means by eternal life. If the church is going to say, "I believe," then it must not try to say, "I believe, but I will believe better if someone will show me the real dope." To believe means exactly what it says: that you believe, confess, and teach. A great secular world will not be impressed by these efforts to shore up the meaning and truth of the Christian faith by a kind of evidence that makes belief unnecessary.

Intellectually, I cannot put any content into the word *live* with regard to the time after I die. Because the only life I know is the finite one that I live before dying. I certainly don't want to do this all over again. I definitely do not want to continue to love the present carcass into all eternity. That is an absurd and not at all pleasant idea. But what life beyond death might be, I have no notion. If all life is engendered and created by God, then that relationship will not be destroyed by the periodic appearance and disappearance of this particular person with my name. Something continues, but what that will be I'm perfectly willing to leave in the hands of the Originator.

Sources

Pages

11–12   Augustana Lutheran Church *Grace Note*, December 1974.

13   Robert M. Herhold, ed., *Probings by Sittler* (Chicago: Lutheran School of Theology at Chicago, 1979), pp. 19–20.

14   Center for the Study of Campus Ministry Yearbook 1977–78.

15   Interview with Robert M. Herhold, October 1975.

16   *Probings*, p. 21.

17–19   *Probings*, pp. 42–47.

20   *Probings*, p. 20.

21   *Oregon Statesman*, October 1978.

22–23   *Chicago Lutheran Seminary Record*, July-October 1945, pp. 22–23.

24   CSCM Yearbook, p. 20.

25–26   *Partners*, June 1979, p. 7.

27   CSCM Yearbook, p. 33.

28   *Chicago Lutheran Seminary Record*, April 1947.

29   *Partners*, p. 9.

30–33   *Chicago Lutheran Seminary Record*, July 1953, pp. 13–15.

34   *The Christian Century*, September 26, 1979, p. 915.

35–36   *The Lutheran*, June 9, 1937; *Chicago Lutheran Seminary Record*, October 1948; *Partners*, pp. 8–9.

37   *Partners*, p. 8.

38   CSCM Yearbook, p. 37.

39   CSCM Yearbook, p. 45.

40–41   Ibid.

42–44   *Motive*, November 1957, pp. 16–17.

45–46   *Chicago Lutheran Seminary Record*, April 1949.

47–56   *The Care of the Earth and Other Sermons* (Philadelphia: Fortress Press, 1964), pp. 75–87.

57–68   *The Ecology of Faith: The New Situation in Preaching* (Philadelphia: Fortress Press, 1961), pp. 76–88.

69–70   "The Structure of Christian Ethics," in *Christian Social Responsibility*, ed. Harold C. Letts, vol. 3, *Life in Community* (Philadelphia: Muhlenberg Press, 1957), pp. 4–6.

71–73   Ibid., pp. 15–17, 36, 38.
74–76   Augustana Lutheran Church *Grace Note,* 1975.
77–78   "The Structure of Christian Ethics," pp. 55–56.
79–80   *Essays on Nature and Grace* (Philadelphia: Fortress Press, 1972), pp. 93–95.
81–85   Ibid., pp. 102–105.
86–91   Ibid., pp. 117–22.
92–95   From "An Aspect of American Religious Experience," an address delivered at the annual meeting of the Catholic Theological Society of America in June 1971.
   96   CSCM Yearbook, p. 41.
   97   Ibid.
98–99   *Probings,* pp. 17–18.
  100   CSCM Yearbook, p. 33.
101–2   *Chicago Lutheran Seminary Record,* April 1954.
103–6   *Probings,* pp. 22–25.
  107   Ibid., pp. 55–56.
108–10   Ibid., pp. 33–35.
  111   Ibid., p. 4.
112–13   Ibid., pp. 48–49.
114–15   World Council of Churches Assembly, New Delhi, 1961.
116–18   *Chicago Lutheran Seminary Record,* October 1949; *Probings,* p. 64.
119–21   *Probings,* pp. 57–61.

The Author

Joseph Sittler is the theologian who, according to Martin E. Marty, "anticipated today's concern for nature, earth, created order, and ecology." These concerns are reflected in his many books: *The Doctrine of the Word* (1948), *The Structure of Christian Ethics* (1958), *The Ecology of Faith* (1961), *The Care of the Earth* (1964), *The Anguish of Preaching* (1967), and *Essays on Nature and Grace* (1972).

Born in Upper Sandusky, Ohio, on September 26, 1904, Joseph Sittler is a graduate of Wittenberg University (1927) and Hamma Divinity School (1930). Many schools and universities—including Lutheran, Roman Catholic, and Unitarian institutions—have awarded him honorary doctorates.

Dr. Sittler was pastor of Messiah Lutheran Church, Cleveland Heights, Ohio (1930–43), and lectured in theology at Oberlin College (1942) prior to coming to Maywood, Illinois, in 1943 to teach systematic theology at the Chicago Lutheran Theological Seminary (now the Lutheran School of Theology at Chicago). From 1957 until his retirement in 1973 he was professor of theology at the divinity school of the University of Chicago.

Professor Sittler served as president of the American Theological Society in 1951 and has been a member of the Academic Council of the Ecumenical Institute for Advanced Theological Study (Jerusalem, 1964–73) and a member of the Commission on Faith and Order of the World Council of Churches (1958–66). He has been a delegate to several Lutheran World Federation and World Council of Churches conferences, and his sermon at a WCC meeting in New Delhi in 1961 is considered one of the theological landmarks of contemporary Christianity. He was chairman of the National Committee to Repeal the McCarran Act (1966–72), which act was ruled unconstitutional in 1974.

One of America's best-known preachers, Sittler has preached in the chapels of a host of colleges and universities in the United States. He has also preached in Italy, France, Germany, England, and the Soviet Union. His lectureships have included the Lyman Beecher (Yale,

1959), the William Belden Noble (Harvard, 1959), the Gray (Duke, 1963), and the Earl (Pacific School of Religion, 1968). Since 1973 Sittler has been a guest lecturer at the Lutheran School of Theology at Chicago. He also travels widely for speaking engagements.

Dr. Sittler and his wife, musician-composer Jeanne, are the parents of six children and reside in Chicago.